THE REAL READER'S QUARTERLY

Slightly Foxed

'Beside the Seaside'

D1500393

NO.75 AUTUMN 2022

Editors: Gail Pirkis & Hazel Wood
Editorial & submissions: Anna Kirk
Marketing & publicity: Steph Allen, Jennie Harrison Bunning & Hattie Summers
Subscriptions, orders & bookshops: Jess Dalby

Cover illustration: Harriet Bane, *Harvest Mouse* (detail)

Born in Bath, Harriet now lives and works in Guernsey. She trained at Wimbledon School of Art, where she received a BA (Hons) in Stage and Theatre Design. Her carefully constructed compositions of wildlife and rural landscapes continue to evolve from her early training in theatre design. To form the surface of her paintings, she applies layers of plaster on board to build texture, followed by a layer of acrylic paint on which the watercolour is worked. Layering in this way allows her more flexibility with the paint, enabling her to build it up or wash it away. Her work is influenced by the artwork of the nineteenth-century recorders of natural history, in particular John James Audubon. To see more of her work visit www.jonathancooper.co.uk.

Design by Octavius Murray
Layout by Andrew Evans
Colophon, tailpiece and back cover fox by David Eccles

© The contributors 2022

Published by Slightly Foxed Limited
53 Hoxton Square
London N1 6PB

tel 020 7033 0258
email office@foxedquarterly.com
www.foxedquarterly.com

Slightly Foxed is published quarterly in early March, June, September and December

Annual subscription rates (4 issues)
UK and Ireland £48; Overseas £56

Single copies of this issue can be bought for £12.50 (UK) or £14.50 (Overseas)

All back issues in printed form are also available

ISBN 978-1-910898-73-4
ISSN 1742-5794

Printed and bound by Smith Settle, Yeadon, West Yorkshire

Contents

Contents

Clare Curtis

The Slightly Foxed Podcast

A new episode of our podcast is available on the 15th of April, July, October and January. To listen, visit www.foxedquarterly.com/pod or search for Slightly Foxed on Audioboom, Apple Podcasts or your podcast app.

Subscriber Benefits

Slightly Foxed can obtain any books reviewed in this issue, whether new or second-hand. To enquire about a book, access the digital edition of *Slightly Foxed* or view a list of membership benefits, visit www.foxedquarterly.com/members or contact the office: 020 7033 0258/office@foxedquarterly.com.

From the Editors

The first crisp feel of autumn in the air is always exciting and somehow unexpected. Old tapes begin to play bringing back memories of new school terms and fresh beginnings, and the prospect of cosy dark evenings with the curtains drawn – though this year for many of us the cosiness is more likely to come from putting on an extra jumper than by turning up the heating.

Here at Slightly Foxed, autumn is one of our busiest times as our lovely, hard-working office team get ready for the Christmas rush. If you too already have Christmas in mind and someone who enjoys diaries on your present list, it's worth taking note of this season's Slightly Foxed Edition, *Nella Last's War* (see p.12). Identified at the time she wrote it simply by her age and occupation: 'Housewife, 49', Nella Last kept her diary as part of the Mass Observation project launched in 1937 to record the lives of ordinary people in Britain. Though she may have been classed as an ordinary housewife living in Barrow-in-Furness, Nella was an extraordinary human being, and her diary gives us a wonderfully vivid picture of everyday life in wartime Britain and the liberation it brought to women like her.

This season's Plain Foxed Edition – our series in which we reissue popular titles no longer available as SFEs in a matching but slightly plainer format – is Graham Greene's *A Sort of Life*. Greene once said that writing this memoir of his early life was 'in the nature of a psychoanalysis' and certainly the character who emerges is as complex and intriguing as any of those he created in his novels. But what marked Greene out above all else was his utter determination to pursue his craft. There can be no more fascinating or illuminating account of what it takes to become a writer.

On the subject of writing, the feeling's been coming over us that it's time for another of our Writer's Competitions. We've greatly benefited from them in the past, finding, predictably, that among our readers there are some very good writers. So why not throw your hat into the ring, and send us a personal piece of not more than 1,500 words that reflects your own experience of a favourite book and that makes other people want to read it too? The winner will receive £250 and the piece will be published in *Slightly Foxed*, while the runner-up will appear on our website. Entries should reach us by 15 January 2023. For more information see our website www.foxedquarterly.com/slightly-foxed-writing-competition (now, incidentally, redesigned and we hope clearer and more user-friendly), or phone us at the office.

And finally, something else to chew over. It's almost twenty years now since, with Steph, we started *Slightly Foxed*. Fortunately we're both still firing on all cylinders (we think!), but as the years have piled up and Slightly Foxed has grown, so, inevitably, have our various commitments, both in and out of the office. We both dearly love editing *Slightly Foxed*, but we're agreed that a little regular freelance help wouldn't come amiss, and the first and most obvious place to look for it seemed to be via our readership. We're on the lookout for a rather special person, probably in their forties or fifties, with solid experience in publishing or journalism or both, to take some of the weight of the things we regularly do. If you would like to know more, please email us at anna@foxedquarterly.com and we'll be in touch.

GAIL PIRKIS & HAZEL WOOD

Beside the Seaside

GALEN O'HANLON

There is something timeless about the British seaside holiday. When I was a child we'd visit my grandparents, who had a beach hut at Studland on the Dorset coast. I would spend happy afternoons playing elaborate games in the sand, interrupted only by Granny leaping from the beach hut in her skirted bathing suit, calling out to me: 'Galey darling, we are going for a swim!' This would fill me with terror: I had still not yet learnt to swim. 'Nonsense!' she'd say, diving in. When I refused to go further than mid-shin, she'd put a thumb to her nose and surge off in a no-nonsense breaststroke. This daily ordeal taught me that a family holiday by the sea is not a straightforwardly happy affair: there are always, as my mum would say, good bits and bad bits.

No writer has captured the seaside holiday as perfectly as R. C. Sherriff. He is best known for his play about the First World War, *Journey's End*, first performed in 1928 and a near-instant success. After such a smash hit he faced the daunting task of what to write next. 'Plays were done with,' he writes in his autobiography, so it would have to be a novel. But all his previous attempts at novel-writing had ended in the bin. In trying to ape the high literary style of the 1920s, he'd floundered with unfamiliar words that wouldn't fit together. Then one day, on a seaside holiday at Bognor, an idea came to him as he sat on the front watching an endless stream of people walk by.

R. C. Sherriff, *The Fortnight in September* (1931)
Persephone · Pb · 336pp · £12 · ISBN 9781906462222

I began to pick out families at random and imagine what their lives were like at home; what hopes and ambitions the fathers had; whether the mothers were proud of their children or disappointed in them; which of the children would succeed and which would go with the tide and come to nothing.

He resolved to pick one of these families at random and build a story around them. 'I wanted to write about simple, uncomplicated people doing normal things.' And the best way to do that was to write about them 'in the simple, uncomplicated words that they would use themselves'. The result was *The Fortnight in September* (1931), a remarkable and uplifting book about a very normal family on a seaside holiday in the 1920s.

The story is effortlessly simple. Mr and Mrs Stevens go to Bognor with their three children: a grown-up daughter Mary who works in a dressmaker's, a son Dick who has just started in a London office, and a young boy, Ernie, who is still at school. They catch the train, stay at a shabby guest house, rent a beach hut, listen to a band and bathe in the sea. On the outside, nothing really happens – summarizing the plot threatens to dissolve it entirely – but the internal lives of the characters are so richly drawn, their emotions so sympathetically articulated, their hopes and anxieties captured in such subtle and simple prose, that the effect is utterly captivating.

Mr Stevens would be the first to tell you that there is a lot more to a holiday than the beach and the sunshine. First there is the house to organize, for which he has a list, half-jokingly called 'Marching Orders', with tasks for everyone to complete before they go. The canary must be dropped off with a neighbour, the little window is to be left ajar for the cat, and the key left with a retired police officer and his wife who live opposite. The Marching Orders have been honed over many years, and Mr Stevens takes great pleasure in having everything in hand.

Then there is the journey to Bognor, which Sherriff elevates to a finely crafted comedic set piece. 'Clapham Junction is perfectly all right if you keep your head,' it begins, before following Mrs Stevens's thoughts as she imagines the ways in which everything might go wrong. Supposing the porters don't get the trunk out? What if she drops the thermos flask, as she did years ago? Is there enough time to change platforms? This is the worst part of the holiday for her: 'Hell, to Mrs Stevens, would be a white-hot Clapham Junction with devils in peaked caps.' She can scarcely believe it when they get through without a single mishap – due, of course, to Mr Stevens's steady and authoritative handling of the situation. She admires him as one would a great hero: 'Clapham Junction seemed to draw from him a mysterious power.' Then Sherriff expertly shifts the viewpoint and we are given this delightful insight:

> Mr Stevens was thinking about himself in the same way. He was conscious of it – this instinctive power – leadership, he supposed it was. His ordinary life gave little chance to draw upon it. It required a Clapham Junction or a burst pipe to bring it to the surface.

Meanwhile, Ernie is entirely unaware of the anxious drama playing out for the adults, apart from wondering why his mother looks rather pale and ill. For him, getting the train is the very peak of excitement. Everything about the railway is designed to whet the appetite but never appease it. There are all the signs declaring danger behind every door, hazards around every corner – none of them explained. Even simple things like the ticket office are baffling: 'For years he had wondered how they got the man through that tiny opening from which he served the tickets. Was he pushed in as a baby – or built in at a later period in his life?' And when he sees a man reloading an automatic ticket machine, which involves unlocking a secret drawer and emptying a shower of pennies into a bag, he resolves from that day onwards to be one of those men: 'It seemed to him the perfection of earthly employment.' This career ambition

remains unshaken until, one night at the bandstand in Bognor, the glory of the bandmaster completely reshapes his world:

> Ernie could not take his eyes off him, suddenly the men who shot the showers of pennies from automatic machines into small black bags became sweating, labouring little animals in paltry jobs. Why had he never realized before that to be a band-master was the one and only thing for him to do?

Part of the book's charm lies in Sherriff's deep sympathy for his characters. We tread side by side with each in turn, seeing the world as they see it, feeling it as they do. And so we discover that Mrs Stevens doesn't enjoy these holidays, even after the ordeal of the train journey is over. The Stevens first came to Bognor for their honeymoon, where they took apartments at 'Seaview' (so called because 'from the lavatory window you could see the top of a lamp post on the front'), and they have returned every year since. But for Mrs Stevens, 'only the honeymoon had been lovely: the coming of the children had made the fortnight a burden – sometimes a nightmare.' She is anxious and withdrawn on holiday. The sea frightens her, never more so than when it's dead calm. The children, too, are different. They laugh at her on holiday in a way they never do at home. The only real pleasure she gets from it is the final hour before bed each night, when she is left alone with her knitting and a glass of port – a holiday luxury, a guilty extravagance.

This is in sharp contrast to Mr Stevens, who looks forward to the holiday as an escape and release: 'The man on his holidays becomes the man he might have been, the man he could have been, had things worked out a little differently.' He can forget the ledgers and invoices of his job as clerk, and instead let his skin go brown in the sunshine as he wanders hatless across the downs behind Bognor.

It is a spacious, relaxed time for the rest of the family, too. Ernie gets the unhindered bliss of days on the beach with his kite and toy yacht, and often falls asleep at supper. Dick gets the space he needs to reflect on his life after school, and his miserable first year at work. And Mary, who is timid and a little shy at home, makes a rather glamorous friend, Jessica, who takes her out on the promenade one evening. There Mary meets Pat Mackenzie, an actor doing a week in rep at the theatre. The romance flutters to life, with all the hesitation and turmoil that comes before the first touch, the first kiss. Although there is no suggestion of it lasting longer than the holiday, these are some of her 'golden hours of life'.

The holiday unfolds exactly as you might expect: there is a rainy morning that clears to a brilliant, sparkling afternoon. They spend hot days in the shade of their beach hut, and Mr Stevens feels glad that he paid more for one with a little balcony. In writing so simply about these normal things, Sherriff beautifully captures a holiday that is absolutely of its time (complete with charabanc rides). And yet he also uncovers the simple, universal truths of what it will always feel like to be on holiday. As you leave the house, you will always wonder if you closed the window in the lavatory. It will always be boring but important to unpack the suitcase on the first day, when really you want to go straight down to the sea. And on that first evening, with the whole holiday before you, you will dream, as Mr Stevens does, of the things you might see and do, and know at the same time that soon it will all be seen and done, and you will look back, from the final evening of the holiday, and wonder how it could be over so quickly.

GALEN O'HANLON lives in London, and dreams of going to the seaside by charabanc.

An Extraordinary Ordinary Housewife

YSENDA MAXTONE GRAHAM

To her readers at the headquarters of the Mass Observation organization in London, she was merely a number (diarist 5353), an occupation (housewife), and an age (49). The labelling was bureaucratic and impersonal, but it was this very anonymity that gave Nella Last (1889–1968) the psychological freedom to tell the truth about her life, making her wartime diaries the raw, revealing testimony that they are.

In a moment of rashness in 1937, she had responded to a request for ordinary people all over Britain to record their daily experiences so that the Government could keep tabs on national morale. 'Housewife, 49' from Barrow-in-Furness was one of the 500 or so applicants invited to join the diary-writing scheme.

Some of them started enthusiastically but soon gave up. Not Nella. From day one, she resolved to fit into her life, along with the usual drudgery of being cook and skivvy for her husband and their two visiting young adult sons, the dashing off of 1,000 words a day on flimsy sheets of A5, which she tied up with string and posted to London each Friday. She would keep up this daily habit till 1966, producing twelve million words in total, making her one of the longest-running and most prolific of the Mass Observation diarists, up there with the accountant in Sheffield who kept going till 1965 and the housewife in Otley, Yorkshire, who kept going till 1967.

It was a rash act to offer her services because her shopfitter husband William (whom she never names) clearly disapproved. Glimpses of his controlling behaviour seep out of these pages, building up an unsettling portrait of a long, dreary imprisonment of a marriage. To write daily anonymous diaries was a quietly subversive way for Nella to put out a call to the outside world.

'Well, you said you wanted an account of my daily life, Mass Observation,' one can hear her thinking, 'and you're jolly well going to get it.' In her forward-sloping handwriting, she lays out her life on a plate: the daily tasks, the love of her sons, the putting up of the Morrison shelter in the dining-room, plus what she cooks for supper ('braised lamb's hearts with whole tiny onions and lots of hot toast' when her son Cliff comes to visit), and how her head feels 'as if it was full of broken glass instead of thoughts' on the day of the Fall of France, how her husband doesn't bother to give her a single thing for Christmas, not even a card, and how just as she thinks she is about to die in a bombing raid she regrets never having got round to opening the last tin of fruit salad.

It's clear she has no idea how good a writer she is. 'Next to being a mother,' she writes, 'I'd have liked to write books – that is if I'd the brains and time.' To which I want to reply, 'Nella, you *are* writing a book! With every pin-sharp observation, you are immortalizing yourself, preserving details of daily life that would otherwise have been lost, and assuring yourself a place in the canon. You do have the brains; and look – by some miracle, although you're also running a household on a mean little budget, literally warming your husband's slippers for him, and managing to make nine babies' nightdresses and fourteen bed-coats out of Winceyette offcuts from the Women's Voluntary Service Centre, you are finding the time to write.'

Did she sit up in bed in her 'semi jerry-built modern house' (as she describes her home with its vegetable garden at 9 Ilkley Road) to scribble out the day's events beside her sleeping husband, or did she write at the kitchen table? I imagine her at the latter, and so did Victoria Wood, who played her in her own 2006 drama *Housewife, 49*, a must-watch after you've read this book. Wood captures perfectly the slightly stooped gait of the housewife who, at last, is unbending herself and spreading her wings, thanks to two things: the catharsis of writing the daily diaries, and the astonishing new freedom of being allowed to be useful in the outside world, which the war brought to her and countless women like her.

Here's a glimpse of that new freedom, written after a day working at the WVS Centre. 'Several times I've not had the tea quite ready when my husband comes in on a Tuesday or a Thursday, and I've felt quite unconcerned.' Her lack of concern highlights the fact that her husband wouldn't have put up with it if she'd behaved like this before the war. 'Gosh, how I've nearly broken my neck to race home in time to brew the tea and pour it.'

Everyone who reads these diaries will be nourished and informed by them in different ways, because they contain so many strands, all the way from the international situation, via the good works of the local ladies, to the spring cleaning, but for me it was Nella's husband's expectation that his home should be run like a hotel by his docile, stay-at-home wife that really stood out. His reasoning: 'I feed you, and clothe you, don't I? I've got a right to say what you do.' This attitude, Nella dares to write in her diary, 'is not love, it's sheer poverty of mind and fear of life.' Her husband, who is actually the frightened one, has kept his wife in a state of fear. These diaries give us a first-hand glimpse of how the war rescued wives from exactly this kind of imprisoned drudgery.

The fact that Nella is clearly 'no ordinary housewife' reminds us that no one is or has ever been 'an ordinary housewife'. Each one, through all the ages, has had her own flame burning beneath the surface: her poetry, her sensitivity, her awareness of the life she would like to have lived.

Even Nella's adored younger son Cliff affectionately calls her 'our dumb blonde'. It's just a joke, but I wanted to scream, 'It's not funny, Cliff!' But oh, how she loves him. He's her true kindred spirit, a gentle, loving, artistic soul. (He will emigrate to Australia after the war and become a sculptor.) Thank goodness Cliff exists – otherwise, one feels, Nella would be utterly psychologically alone, with her undemonstrative husband and her narrow-minded, fault-finding in-laws. 'Don't change,' Cliff implores her. 'Let other women grow hard – you keep nice and soft.' Her second-favourite person in the world is her elder son Arthur, but she can't disguise the fact that Cliff is her favourite.

Cliff fights in the war, and Nella is sickened at the thought of it. Yes, she is 'soft' – too soft, she realizes. She admits she seems to have 'a skin less' than other people and is haunted to the point of nightmares by the injuries and deaths of people in the town when it is bombed. One day her husband tells her that she sobbed bitterly in her sleep. But when he says, 'I want my boy safe,' she shakes (again) with rage. 'Safe for what?' she retorts. 'Till his soul dies in his body, and even his body goes back on him with repeated nervous breakdowns, and bitter inward thoughts turn his blood sour and cripple and torment him?'

In other words, she is no pacifist: she believes 'we must all play our own game as the cards are dealt'. Talking of dealing cards, she likes to read Tarot cards (one reading tells her 'You will sit alone with sadness in a crowd'), and she also likes to have her fortune told. A gypsy called Madame Curl at Blackpool has foretold the bomb blast that will damage her house.

And talking of beliefs, you may well be shocked in these pages by some of the Last family's convictions. This diary is a snapshot of what people were really, truly, genuinely thinking, and my jaw did drop a few times. For example, while on the one hand Nella looks at her own honey-coloured tiled fireplace 'with a wonder that is like reverence' when she thinks of the Jewish mothers in Europe having to leave their homes, Arthur reveals himself to be a casual anti-Semite. 'I think I've got the Manchester outlook on Jews,' he remarks one day. 'A parasitic people who live "on" rather than "with" others.'

Nella's husband listens to Lord Haw-Haw's broadcasts from

Germany, coming to bed 'with his eyes starting out of his head with nerves and worry'. And Nella writes on 19 January 1941 (brace yourself for this), 'I never thought I'd admire Hitler, but today when I read in the *Sunday Express* that he "painlessly gassed" some thousands of lunatics, I did so. I believe firmly in euthanasia in incurable cases, whether of cancer etc. or of mind disease.' Golly – it's one thing to contemplate putting her dog Sol down to spare him the terror of the Blitz (and she actually decides not to carry this out, on seeing his dear little wagging tail the next morning) but quite another to applaud Hitler's T4 Euthanasia Programme.

Prepare yourself too for the Great Gap in these diaries. A chunk is missing, presumed destroyed. We go straight from Christmas 1943 to May 1945 – so, no D-Day, no Arnhem, no slow grind through the last year and a half of the war. I asked Jessica Scantlebury, who curates the Mass Observation archive at the University of Sussex, what on earth happened, and she told me that some of the collection got lost, perhaps disposed of after water-damage, or 'perhaps it was simply not packed up when the Archive moved to Sussex in the early 1970s'.

So, for us and for all the marvellous women who work with Nella at the WVS Centre and at the Red Cross canteen for men manning the anti-aircraft guns (they all call each other Mrs this and Miss that, and never use first names), all too soon it's the end of the war, and the Centre will soon close. Miss Heath, with whom Nella has worked for five happy years, says, 'Lasty, I'm going to miss you more than I realized.' Nella is certainly going to miss her, and the work. She is full of dread. 'I will not, cannot go back to the narrowness of my husband's "I don't want anyone else's company but yours – why do you want anyone else?"' On going home, she writes, 'I looked at his placid, blank face and marvelled at the way he had managed to dominate me for all our married life.'

But then, out of nowhere, her husband makes what almost counts as a grateful remark. 'By Jove, when I hear some men talking about what they get to eat, I realize how lucky I am.' To which Nella responds (in her diary, though, not out loud), 'Thirty years of marriage and two wars for that remark.'

As this part of her diary comes to a close in August 1945 it's time for leisure again. Petrol rationing will end, and the two of them, tired out and with hair greying, will at last be able to resume their regular Sunday outings to Coniston Water in the Lake District, a place Nella loves and from which she draws strength and calm.

This extraordinary ordinary housewife's can-do attitude should be an inspiration to us all. One day in January 1940, for example, out of the blue, her local doctor knocks on the door and delivers a minuscule baby to her in a brown paper bag. It's premature, and he needs her to look after it for a week, as its parents are ill and its granny dying. Nella takes in the baby (a girl), tucks it up in a lined drawer, and feeds it Nestlé's milk on the hour every hour: just one more task in her very full to-do list.

That doctor was right: Nella Last's your woman, when you need motherly wisdom, instant practical help and a hot supper, and when you need to win a war.

YSENDA MAXTONE GRAHAM is keen to cycle round Barrow Island, also known as the Furness Peninsula, and find Nella's house at 9 Ilkley Road, which you can see on Google Maps. Author of three Slightly Foxed titles, including *Terms & Conditions*, Ysenda's forthcoming book, *Jobs for the Girls: How Young Women Made their Way in the World of Work, 1945–1990*, will be published next year.

Nella Last's War: The Second World War Diaries of Housewife, 49 (392pp) is now available in a limited and numbered cloth-bound edition of 2,000 copies (subscribers: UK & Eire £18, Overseas £20; non-subscribers: UK & Eire £20, Overseas £22). All prices include post and packing. Copies may be ordered by post (53 Hoxton Square, London N1 6PB), by phone (020 7033 0258) or via our website www.foxedquarterly.com.

Gaslight and Newgate Knockers

PATRICK WELLAND

Literary associations with drugs abound: Samuel Taylor Coleridge and Thomas De Quincey (opium); Jean-Paul Sartre and W. H. Auden (Benzedrine); Charles Baudelaire and William Butler Yeats (hashish); William Burroughs (the lot). Then there are the drunks, a list of whose names would take up the rest of this page.

What was the effect of these stimulants? Robert Louis Stevenson reputedly wrote *The Strange Case of Dr Jekyll and Mr Hyde* during a six-day cocaine binge. A good thing. The alcoholic F. Scott Fitzgerald admitted that organizing and revising a long book 'do not go well with liquor'. A bad thing. But, for better or worse, these authors at least knew what to expect when they swallowed, sniffed, smoked or shot up their drug of choice.

Gravely ill, Michael Cox was taken unawares.

For thirty years Cox, a senior commissioning editor at the Oxford University Press, was obsessed with writing a pastiche Victorian sensation novel but he failed to progress further than a few discarded drafts. Then, in 2004, aged 56, he started to lose his sight as a result of a rare cancer. To reduce pressure on his optic nerve, he was given the steroid dexamethasone. Astonishingly, this fired him to start afresh his oft-abandoned novel with such intense mental and physical energy that he wrote the first 30,000 words in eight weeks.

Over the next seventeen months, Cox produced his atmospheric

Michael Cox, *The Meaning of Night: A Confession* (2006) · John Murray · Pb · 608pp · £10.99 · ISBN 9780719568374; *The Glass of Time: A Novel* (2008) · John Murray · Pb · 544pp · £7.99 · ISBN 9780719596902.

The Meaning of Night: A Confession (2006). He said: 'I was buzzing with ideas, hyperactive and unable to sleep. Subconsciously, I felt I may go blind and that if I don't do this now, I'll never do it.' On completion, the 600-page book was auctioned in a publishing bidding war for £430,000. But Cox was not finished. With his sight and health still deteriorating, he wrote a sequel, the equally lengthy *The Glass of Time: A Novel*, published in 2008. He died a year later.

I knew nothing of this when I found a copy of *The Meaning* in a charity shop. However, favourable comparisons with Wilkie Collins suggested an enjoyable immersion in melodramatic waters. Any further doubts about the purchase (how many doubts can you have for £2?) were dispelled by the arresting opening sentence: 'After killing the red-haired man, I took myself off to Quinn's for an oyster supper.'

In an Editor's Preface, J. J. Antrobus, 'Professor of Post Authentic Victorian Fiction at Cambridge University', tells us that *The Meaning* is the unreliable memoir of Edward Glyver, transcribed from a recently discovered manuscript. Each of the manuscript's forty-seven sections is headed by a Latin title: *hinc illae lacrimae* (hence these tears), *alea iacta est* (the die is cast), *resurgam* (I shall rise again) and so on. Footnotes throughout allude to Victorian personalities, London geography, the meaning of now forgotten words, family lineages and obscure books, both real and fictional. Cox, it is clear, knows the times of which he writes, as is to be expected of the biographer of M. R. James and co-editor of *The Oxford Book of Victorian Ghost Stories*.

The manuscript describes Glyver's obsessive attempt to reclaim the destiny of which he has been cheated. Our hero is an equivocal man to lead us on such a quest. A bibliophile and scholar, he is sentimental and loyal to those he loves. Yet he is also an opium addict ('Confession' in the subtitle mirrors De Quincey's *Confessions of an English Opium-Eater*), a client of prostitutes, an unprincipled legal agent and a predator who, plotting murder, butchers a stranger before setting out on his quest to prove he is capable of the act. Glyver's consuming desire for vengeance has driven him insane.

The deciphering of his mother's diaries and notebooks after her death leads Glyver to the honest lawyer Tredgold and the realization that he has been betrayed and so deprived of a prize beyond measure. Piece by piece the complex jigsaw of deception is assembled, and past mysteries – the fleeting touch of an unseen stranger's hand, a rosewood box left for the child Glyver by a woman whose name he never knew, the significance of the words *sursum corda* (lift up your hearts), from the Latin Eucharist, contained in a letter – are resolved.

You can almost sense Cox's delight at being released from three decades of creative frustration as he draws on his encyclopaedic knowledge of the Victorian era to portray 1850s London in all its hypocrisy, violence and gaudy vulgarity. The cobbled, gaslit streets; the inspissated fog that turns passers-by into 'shuffling phantoms'; the reeking rookeries; the scented courtesans in their brocaded 'academies of love'; the fraudsters, toolers (pickpockets) and rampsmen (muggers); a world in which rogues sport Newgate knockers (heavily greased side whiskers swept back to the ears) and carry Dickensian names such as Josiah Pluckrose and Fordyce Jukes. And ever in the background is the shape-shifting figure of Phoebus Rainsford Daunt, who earned Glyver's hatred as a youth and comes to dominate his mind.

Here is our dubious protagonist – both victim and villain – listless in an opium den. Yielding to the fumes, he reveals his Janus nature, hovering between light and darkness:

> The boundaries of this world are ever shifting – from day to night, joy to sorrow, and from life itself to death . . . I have been given my own ever-changing margins, across which I move, continually and hungrily, like a migrating animal. Now civilized, now untamed; now responsive to decency and human concern, now viciously attuned to the darkest of desires . . . if these acts disgust you, then it must be so.

Reflecting this schizophrenia, Glyver's trail leads him from the stews of London to the faery splendour of Evenwood Park in Northamptonshire, seat of the forbidding Julius Verney Duport, 25th Baron Tansor, 'a man in whom disapproval and suspicion of his fellow human beings was instinctive and irreversible'. Inevitably, beneath Evenwood's six cupola-topped towers sinister currents flow. Lord Tansor's young wife Laura has died, driven mad by her guilt at a terrible secret act. Tansor has remarried but is tormented by lack of a male heir. In this brooding atmosphere, Glyver fatally falls in love with the enigmatic Emily Carteret and reacquaints himself with the egregious Daunt, by now a fêted (in Glyver's opinion, execrable) poet who has insinuated himself into Lord Tansor's favour. A second betrayal, even more shocking than the first, awaits the reader before a denouement in the midst of a Park Lane gathering of Victorian high society.

Erudite, excursive and written in elaborate prose that is a pitch-perfect reflection of the Victorian age, this tapestry of murder, love, vengeance, providence and perfidy is in the grand tradition of those luxuriously lengthy novels in which our forebears lost themselves when leisure time was spent reading instead of watching box sets. Characters are properly fleshed out with their own fateful back stories, interwoven relationships are unstitched, and there is the occasional happy coincidence to push the plot along. But perhaps the most important character is the Victorian world itself, recreated by an author whose love and knowledge of the time shine through. And if you think the ending is a trifle abrupt, almost as if the author has unfinished business . . .

The Glass picks up the story twenty years later in 1876 with the arrival at Evenwood of 19-year-old orphan Esperanza Gorst. Esperanza has been raised in France by her guardian, Madame L'Orme, who has contrived for her to be hired as personal maid to the widowed Lady Tansor. She is told by Madame only that she must gain Lady Tansor's complete trust so she can fulfil a 'Great Task'. The nature of the Task is initially withheld, for such knowledge might influence her natural, generous character and so lay her open to suspicion. Once established in Lady Tansor's affections, she will be given more information and advice by Madame in intermittent Letters of Instruction.

Like any proper heroine of a Victorian potboiler, Esperanza is soon busily making her own investigations, aided by memoirs and newspaper cuttings sent by Madame. Through her diary, we follow her as she slips through Evenwood's myriad rooms, peering behind pictures, opening drawers and eavesdropping on conversations from a conveniently discovered hideaway. What secret does the housekeeper Mrs Battersby – a splendid Mrs Danvers figure – hide behind her unsettling reticence? We fear for Esperanza as, on a fleeting trip to London, she follows Lady Tansor's lawyer, Augustus Vyse, to a stinking Billingsgate pub where he passes money to a young man with murder in his eyes. Whose hand turns the outside key to release Esperanza from the vaulted mausoleum in which she is later locked? Who is the one-armed man with a chimney-pot hat who regards Evenwood from a distance with such intensity yet clearly wishes not to be seen?

At the heart of these mysteries lies the formidable Lady Tansor, possessor of knowledge so dark that even her own father is killed to preserve its secrecy. Mighty in rank and authority, unflinching and harsh, she can switch in a moment from icy fury to pathetic reliance on Esperanza who, from emotional need, she elevates to the position of her companion. Esperanza must crush any sympathy she feels for this tormented creature, for Madame has warned her: 'She can *never* be your friend . . . her interests and yours are, & will always be, utterly opposed. She is – and always will be – your enemy. Let this be your one guiding principle in everything you do.'

With echoes of *Bleak House* in its Byzantine plot involving inheritance, questions of identity and secrets long held by a titled woman, *The Glass* can be read as a stand-alone mystery, though those who approach it as a sequel will find it equally enjoyable. Readers will soon guess Esperanza's identity and the outline of the 'prize that awaits'. But they will have to wait 333 pages for the Great Task to be laid bare by Madame. And, of course, by that time undreamed-of circumstances imperil its outcome – and there are still another 280 pages to go.

In mad Glyver, we have the dark; in Esperanza, the light piercing a shadowy past which, like a contagion, infects the present. She is young, innocent and curious; artful enough to deceive her elders, brave enough to quell her fears, yet frail enough to doubt her strength and to lose her heart to love. Cox wants us to know the inspiration for such a heroine, as if we need to be told. At the end of another day's labours, Esperanza writes: 'After dressing my Lady for dinner, I returned at last to my room, wrote a long account of the day in my Book, and read a little from Mr Wilkie Collins . . .'

Another Victorian novelist, Charles Reade, author of *The Cloister and the Hearth*, advised 'Make 'em laugh; make 'em cry; make 'em wait.' In that, these two books – really, a single 1,100-page epic – deliciously succeed.

PATRICK WELLAND left Fleet Street twelve years ago to concentrate on doing as little as possible apart from reading and occasional writing.

Seeing the Wood . . .

Some books grow on you. Others help you grow.

In January 1990, aged 24 and not long out of drama school, I landed a job: six months touring an Alan Ayckbourn play round secondary schools in northern Germany. The work was surprisingly rewarding – we soon discovered that German teenagers were, for some reason, hungry for 1970s British class comedy – but downtime was a problem. There was nothing to do.

Our digs tended to be rural B&Bs in the flat, unpromising hinterland between Hamburg and the Danish border, where villages were small and morosely agricultural; few had shops or pubs, and if they did the life in them rarely exceeded one, usually unfriendly, local. My German was passable but not up to enjoying television, and there was nowhere to buy English books. So on my days off, I had a choice. Stay indoors, staring at the paintwork – or go for a walk.

I walked. It was January, it was Germany, and it was the countryside. All there was to look at were empty, muddy fields, and trees. A mass of trees, winter-black, wet and indistinguishable. At first I saw them only in a disconnected, can't-see-the-wood sort of way, but

---

Alastair Fitter and David More, *Trees* (1980) · Collins Gem · Pb · 240pp · £5.99 · ISBN 9780007183067; Thomas Pakenham, *Meetings with Remarkable Trees* (1992) · Weidenfeld & Nicolson · Hb · 192pp · £30 · ISBN 9781474601474; Peter Wohlleben, *The Hidden Life of Trees* (2015) · Collins · Pb · 288pp · £9.99 · ISBN 9780008218430; Martin Crawford, *Creating a Forest Garden* (2010) · Green Books · Pb · 384pp · £24.95 · ISBN 9780857845535; Chris Starr, *Woodland Management* (2005) · Crowood Press · Hb · 192pp · £16.99 · ISBN 9781847976178.

then, soon, I became more curious. What *kind* of trees were they? What were their *names*?

Memories stirred of primary-school lessons pressing leaves between blotting paper, of acorns and catkins laid out on the Nature Table: that tree there, that was an oak; that spiny evergreen was a holly, obviously. But what was that other one, the one with the sticky black buds? Or that one, with bark that glistened like a garnet under water?

In February, my brand-new boyfriend came over from England to visit, and I told him about my walks and the nameless, intriguing trees. A week after he'd gone back home, he sent me a letter, and a book. The letter asked me to move in with him. The book, chosen because it was small enough to fit in an ordinary A5 envelope, was a pocket guide to trees.

*

Trees, by Alastair Fitter, came out in 1980, published by Collins in its 'Collins Gem' format ('small, but packed with stuff'). The first of these little books, each just 3 x 4½ inches, had appeared almost exactly a century earlier, with the advent of the Collins Gem Diary, and was such a hit that Collins had been churning them out ever since. My pocket guide was one of the first in the format's 1980s revamp, with body text in a Gill-ish sans font, a clean, single-photo cover design and, crucially, full-colour illustrations of each of the 229 tree species listed in the contents. The publishers considered these illustrations so important that the title page gives their creator, David More, equal billing with Fitter.

It was the right decision. The book begins '"Tree" is one of those useful words that have no precise definition yet are immediately understood.' Well, that may be true, but using words to describe what makes a species of tree recognizable isn't so simple. Take the English elm (*Ulmus procera*). Fitter describes its leaves as 'small, rounded, rough-surfaced, dark green', but if it hadn't been for the illustration opposite, I'd barely have been able to tell an elm leaf from an unripe plum.

Size matters. The Gem really was a pocket-sized pocket guide, so I could take it out on walks and thumb through those vital illustrations until I saw something that might be a match. In my German winter, when the deciduous trees were still leafless and baffling, I focused on how to tell the needles on a spruce ('stiff, sharp') from a fir ('aromatic, dull'), or the scales on a cedar ('white-streaked') from a cypress ('smell of parsley when crushed'). From the state of the pages, this clearly took a lot of thumbing.

My walks were more profitable now, but winter dragged on. March came and went, then April; still the icy weather. I was homesick, tired of snow, driving the van from village to village, cured meats for breakfast and never a vegetable to eat except potatoes and creamed sweetcorn. I began to long for green: green salad on my plate, green leaves on the trees.

In the last weeks of the job, the tour took us south and east. Finally, gratefully, spring unspooled before us. It was the second week of May when our van reached Berlin, the last stop on the tour.

Berlin is a city that honours chestnuts. Its avenues and parks were exuberant with them, horse (*Aesculus hippocastanum*) and sweet (*Castanea sativa*), all in full, glorious leaf like lime-green chandeliers in the spring sunlight, candled with spires of pink-flushed, foaming flowers. The whole of that final week I walked beneath them, tilting my face up towards the canopies, bathing in the great wash of green. I rang my new boyfriend. Yes, I said; yes thank you, I would like to move in.

The Wall had fallen, I was going home, and I could name trees.

*

Is the naming of things the first step in knowing them? Is the word 'tree', as Alastair Fitter said, 'immediately understood'? In the film *Tolkien* (2019), David Jacobi plays an elderly linguistics professor who tells the young, pre-*Hobbit* J. R. R. that the single word 'oak' contains a multitude of meanings. Oak: that tree you climbed as a child. Oak: a tree you've never seen, where a king once hid. Oak: a timber used to build houses, ships, sideboards. Oak: British hearts of. For him, the act of naming a tree 'oak' is a key that unlocks richness, and when I first turned through the pages of the Gem guide, I agreed: naming a tree meant you knew it. That was all there was to know. Gosh, but I had a lot to learn.

Luckily for those who want to learn about trees, there are plenty of books that can help. Probably the first English-language book on the subject was John Evelyn's *Sylva, or A Discourse of Forest-Trees and the Propagation of Timber in His Majesty's Dominions*, published in 1664 and an immediate hit. Half practical guide to growing trees for money, half celebration of notable individual trees, new editions were regularly published right up until the early twentieth century, and it set the mould for much of what has followed: 300-odd years later, *Meetings with Remarkable Trees* (1992) would pull the same trick, pairing Thomas Pakenham's photographs of ancient specimen trees with his loving pen-portraits.

Sarah Woolfenden, 'Twisted Yew'

In its oddly schizophrenic attitude – Cut 'em down! / Let 'em live! – *Sylva* is typical. Humanity can't seem to decide whether trees are a commodity to be used and discarded, or beings to be venerated and protected. Either way, the faster we cut down trees, the more people seem to want to read about them. In 2015 the journal *Nature* said that 15.3 trillion trees are lost to felling each year. That same year Random House in Germany published a chatty but (you'd think) niche round-up of current forest science, *The Hidden Life of Trees*, by Peter

Wohlleben. An instant bestseller, it would go on to be translated into forty languages.

*

Reader, I married the Gem-giver, then had two sons with him. Eventually we bought a house, one with a piece of land big enough to plant a vegetable garden. And, as it turned out, trees.

My husband was an actual living tree-hugger: as a little boy let out of doors, he would run beaming to the first tree he saw and wrap his arms around the trunk. By now I was a journalist, had a couple of bees co-habiting in my bonnet about climate change and food security, and wanted space and time to try growing enough food to feed my family. Martin Crawford's magisterial *Creating a Forest Garden: Working with Nature to Grow Edible Crops* (2010) was a natural fit.

Forest gardens – where crops grow as part of a matrix of trees, shrubs and herb layers – are an ancient way of producing food in semi-tropical regions. In the 1990s Crawford adapted the practice to suit temperate climates, planting a one-acre forest garden in Devon that now produces, he says, enough to feed nine people, while requiring only minimal management and no outside fertilizers. Having spent a winter double-digging manure into 80 square metres of traditional veg garden, that was an appealing proposition. We went to visit Crawford's site – imagine the garden of Eden, except damper – and then bought the book.

It's sitting next to me now, heavily Sellotaped across the spine, and almost the exact opposite of the Gem guide. Big (27.5 x 22cms), hardback, heavy: the only pocket this would fit would be Brobding-nagian. The cover shows lovely, tree-y things to eat like plums and hazelnuts, plus what I now know is the flower of that odiferous woodlander, wild garlic. Inside, roughly a third of the book discusses how a forest garden works, and how to plant and plan your own. Almost all the remainder is an intensely detailed guide to the growing habits and needs of hundreds of shrubs, perennials and trees. Result? Total greed: I wanted them all.

And so the planting began. We started with Italian alder (*Alnus cordata*), a pioneer tree that eats poor, wet soils for breakfast. Literally: bacteria that live in its roots absorb atmospheric nitrogen and turn it into various forms of soluble nitrates – basically, a full English for plants. Even better, the book said, any spare nitrates the alder produces are transported by fungal threads in the soil to lower-nutrient areas, where other plants can then tuck in.

As a gardener, I already knew that these threads – or mycorrhiza – wrapped around the roots of individual plants and helped them access nutrients in the soil. But this was my first brush with the intriguing notion that they benefited *all* the plants in an area. It seemed some trees, together with their fungal friends, were actively improving their own environment.

For protection from wind (Crawford, like all good gardeners, knows the stunting effect of wind on both people and plants), we next created a shelterbelt, hiving off a semi-circular area of pasture to the north and planting it with 200-odd trees. Species-wise, we spread our bets: holm oak and Scots pine to filter the wind in winter; red oak and English to do the same in summer; hornbeam, sweet chestnut and hazel to coppice for rods and poles; silver birch and spindle to nurse the slower growers; bog myrtle, goat willow and weeping willow to dry out the wet spots; wild cherry and apple for fruits for us; berried holly, rowan, hawthorn and guelder rose for fruits for the birds.

The young trees were just little sticks, a foot or so high; for the first year or two, the ex-field looked like a twig cemetery. Unsure how to nurture tree babies, I read Chris Starr's *Woodland Management: A Practical Guide* (2005) and dutifully followed his advice: watering by hand during the first droughty summer, weeding around the young roots, scattering buckets of chicken manure pellets, loosening tree ties, retying tree ties, pruning out ill-placed branches in winter. Hard, hard work, but, I felt, important.

The trees grew, as trees do. Our family changed, as families do. The boys grumped their way through adolescence; my husband's

Sarah Woolfenden, 'Garlic Wood'

father died, slowly; my father died, suddenly. By then, Home Wood stood tall, the silver birch already 5m, the hybrid poplars 9m or more. We scattered my dad's ashes under three young oaks, looking south across a sunny glade. There was hardly any wind, and his ashes lay quiet; the trees had done their job. I stood there thinking how, in planting them, we had done exactly the right thing. I knew trees' names and now I knew how to look after them. I was in control.

And then our son disappeared . . .

The story of Isabel Lloyd's life with trees will continue in Issue 76.

ISABEL LLOYD is co-author of *Gardening for the Zombie Apocalypse: How to Grow Your Own Food When Civilization Collapses – Or Even if it Doesn't* (2019).

The Dream that Failed

ANTHONY WELLS

Called into the dentist's surgery the other day, I put the book I had been reading in the waiting-room – *The Dream that Failed* (1994) by Walter Laqueur – on a table by the door. The title caught the eye of the dentist's assistant, who asked what it was about. 'The fall of the Soviet Union,' I replied. 'The Soviet Union?' she asked. I was surprised the name meant nothing to her: the assistant, Julia, is Polish, as I had discovered on a previous visit. 'What Russia was called until 1991. Haven't you heard of it?' 'Maybe at school we did,' she replied.

Laqueur's book is largely an investigation of how and why Western observers, including the Sovietologists as they were known, failed to understand the USSR and foresee its collapse. However, it would not be the book I would recommend to Julia to learn about the system that ruled Russia from 1917 to 1991. For that, I would go to a book that showed me the reality of the Soviet Union when I first read it in the 1970s, when the USSR was still going strong (or appeared to be). That book was *Hope against Hope* (1970), by the incomparable Nadezhda Mandelstam.

Nadezhda Mandelstam was born Nadezhda Khazina in the southern Russian town of Saratov, on the Volga, in 1899, into a middle-class Jewish family. Her father was a lawyer and her mother a doctor, one of the first women in Russia to be allowed to qualify. Early in her life the family moved to Kiev, where Nadezhda attended school and then

Nadezhda Mandelstam, *Hope against Hope* (1970) · Harvill · Pb · 448pp · £16.99 · ISBN 9781860466359; *Hope Abandoned* (1974) · Harvill · Pb · 704pp · £25 · ISBN 9781846556548.

studied art. But she is famous not as an artist – she never pursued her career – but as the wife, and widow, of the poet Osip Mandelstam, whom she met in Kiev in 1919 and married soon after; and for the two-volume memoir she wrote clandestinely in the 1960s, remembering her life with her husband and reflecting on the 'catastrophe', as she calls it, that had overtaken them and their friends, acquaintances and contemporaries, and their homeland, since the Bolsheviks seized power.

The first volume of her memoir, *Hope against Hope* (a pun in English on her first name, Nadezhda, which means 'hope' in Russian), opens with an account of her husband's arrest by the secret police in Moscow on the night of 13 May 1934 and ends with an account of how she learned about his death in a transit camp in eastern Siberia and her attempts to ascertain the exact date on which he died (established later as 27 December 1938). In the eighty short chapters between the two, she takes the reader into the heart of Soviet life during those four years, years when the Stalin terror reached its height and tens if not hundreds of thousands of Soviet citizens were arrested, imprisoned, interrogated and either summarily shot or carted off to the camps of what became known as the Gulag.

Nadezhda Mandelstam's memoir is written from the inside of the 'new epoch', by someone who, while not close to the seat of Soviet power, was through her husband well connected to the world of Soviet literature, even though he was ostracized from it. None of Osip Mandelstam's poetry was permitted to appear in print after 1928 and, effectively an 'unperson' from that time on, he survived on what he could earn from translation and the occasional prose piece he could get published. In the late '20s, the intellectual conflict between his understanding of poetry and a need not to be out of step with his times – a need which was leading almost all of his fellow writers to make their pact with the regime – dried up his poetic inspiration. Only in the early '30s did his ability to write poetry return after, in his wife's words, he had 'ceased to regard the new order as the beginning of the millennium' and had 'recovered complete inner freedom'.

In late 1933 Mandelstam used this inner freedom to compose the poem that precipitated his first arrest, the event with which *Hope against Hope* opens. The poem, known as 'The Stalin Epigram', was a biting satirical portrait of the 'great leader', painting a picture of a physically and morally repulsive 'mountain-man' with fingers like grubs and a moustache like the bristles of a cockroach. Mandelstam, as was his habit, read his new poem to a small circle of friends, one of whom – to no one's surprise – turned out to be a police informer. There was, as Nadezhda explains, one among everyone's friends, if not family.

This poem, as someone commented about another of Mandelstam's poems, was 'the kind of thing which would bring three men in uniform knocking on your door'. This it had done. The police agents spent the night searching the apartment, examining any and every poem and piece of paper they turned up (missing some which Nadezhda had sewn into cushions or hidden in saucepans). When morning came, Mandelstam was taken off to the Lubyanka prison, leaving Nadezhda and their friend, the poet Anna Akhmatova, alone in the Moscow apartment. In her third chapter, Nadezhda Mandelstam reflects on how they reacted, and how typical they were of the family and friends of those picked up by 'the organs of state security':

We never asked, on hearing about the latest arrest, 'What was he arrested for?' but we were exceptional. Most people, crazed by fear, asked this question just to give themselves a little hope: if others were arrested for some reason, then they wouldn't be arrested, because they hadn't done anything wrong. They vied with each other in thinking up ingenious reasons to justify each arrest: 'Well, she really is a smuggler, you know' . . . or . . . 'I always thought there was something fishy about him. He isn't one of us at all.' This was enough for anyone to be arrested and destroyed: 'not one of us', 'talks too much', 'a bad character'. . .

variations on a theme we had first heard in 1917 . . . This was why we had outlawed the question, 'What was he arrested for?' '*What for?*' Akhmatova would cry indignantly whenever, infected by the prevailing climate, anyone of our circle asked this question. 'What do you mean, *what for?* It's time you understood that people are arrested *for nothing!*'

This is the technique of *Hope against Hope*, which uses the author's personal experience, and anecdote, as an illustration of the history of her times and a spur to reflection on the causes, especially the intellectual and moral causes, of the Soviet tyranny. Because she experienced this tyranny at first hand, escaping imprisonment and the camps herself only by chance (in late 1938 the secret police came to where she had been living just one day after she had moved elsewhere), her words, delivered with pungency and black humour, and without the least sentimentality or self-pity, convey directly what it was like to live through the disastrous experiment of creating a Communist state. In reading *Hope against Hope*, it is as if you have found yourself in private conversation with her and you realize, after her very first words, that this is someone you have to listen to.

Nadezhda Mandelstam's style is blunt, straight-talking, miraculously free of jargon and Soviet 'newspeak', simultaneously severe and compassionate about those who sold their souls to the new regime. She does not rant or stand in judgement on individuals who made their pact with the devil: it was only too understandable. She even refuses to condemn the person – Vladimir Stavski – who, as head of the Union of Writers, wrote and signed the denunciation of Mandelstam that supplied the pretext for his second arrest and the five-year sentence of 'corrective labour' which led directly to his premature death. (Stavski's denunciation was retrieved from the archives after the fall of the regime in 1991.)

'Any other official would have done the same as Stavski,' Mandelstam writes, unless he wanted to be spirited away by car at the dead of night. We were all the same: either sheep who went willingly to the slaughter, or respectful assistants to the executioners. Whichever role we played, we were uncannily submissive, stifling all our human instincts . . . Crushed by the system each one of us had in some way or other helped to build, we were not even capable of passive resistance.

Nadezhda Mandelstam did not live to see the release of this document, for she died in 1980. Nor did she live to see her own work officially published in her own country: the English translations were made from a text published through the *samizdat* underground publishing system. So she never personally enjoyed the fame her memoirs brought her in the West and remained a more or less invisible figure. Or so I thought at the time I first read the books, in the mid-'70s.

But in 1982, the BBC broadcast a documentary about the Mandelstams. Made by the writer and programme-maker Nigel Williams, it featured the Russian poet Joseph Brodsky and some footage from an interview with Nadezhda filmed in 1973, which was shown for the first time in the UK. Brodsky had been forcibly exiled from the Soviet Union in 1972, after serving part of a sentence of forced labour and then being hounded as persona non grata for his (clandestinely published) poetry and his Jewishness. A magnetic personality on the screen, reading Mandelstam's poetry in Russian and hailing Nadezhda's memoirs as a 'literary masterpiece', Brodsky appears alongside other literary figures of the time. But all, even Brodsky, are eclipsed by the footage of the quietly spoken, dark-eyed, calmly self-assured Nadezhda, who sits slightly hunched in her chair in her Moscow apartment, quite still, puffing occasionally on the Russian *papirosa* cigarette she holds in her right hand, looking unwaveringly at the camera and speaking in accented but fluent English in reply to the (unheard) interviewer's questions.

'Our marriage was sexually very successful,' she says at one point, with the faintest flicker of a smile on her lips. It was, for the time, an extraordinary thing to hear; and it conveys something of the essence of her and her husband's shared understanding of the world. Mandelstam, she explains in the sequel to *Hope against Hope, Hope Abandoned* (1974), thought that 'in the world of human beings . . . everything good and creative was endowed with sex, while everything dead or destructive is sexless . . . [He] was convinced that the basis of life, the source of goodness, and the higher illumination of love were to be found in the intimacy between two people . . .' Hardly a conviction you would have found echoed in official Soviet thought.

After her husband's death, Nadezhda Mandelstam devoted her life to preserving his poetry and then, in her memoirs, preserving the record of his life, their life together and the terrible times through which they had lived. *Hope against Hope* and *Hope Abandoned* are her great testament and, in Brodsky's words, 'a Day of Judgement on earth for her age and its literature'. In them Julia my dentist's assistant will find no better account of what it was like to live through 'the dream that failed'.

ANTHONY WELLS is currently writing a reflection on anti-Semitism inspired by his years at the Wiener Library in London, on whose shelves he first came across *Hope against Hope*. You can also hear him discussing the library in Episode 27 of our podcast.

Monster-hunting

DAVID FLEMING

As a child I had three great ambitions. The first was to go to the South Pole – I practised wandering off to die in a storm like Captain Oates whenever snow fell in the local park. Then there was my wish to roam the London sewers having had a tantalizing glimpse of them in a *Doctor Who* episode. Finally, I longed to see the Loch Ness Monster and to know for sure that it existed. Now somewhat older, I find the thought of sub-zero temperatures has put me off polar exploration, and my zest for sewers is lessened by the prospect of bad smells and rodents. It would, however, still be exciting to behold across the peaty waters of Loch Ness something strange and wonderful, but I rarely give the matter much thought.

Some people, however, remain true to their childhood dreams. From the age of 12 F. W. Holiday had an abiding interest in that most famous of Scottish mysteries. It became an all-consuming fascination and in later life led him to write an oddly titled but persuasive book on the subject – *The Great Orm of Loch Ness* (1968).

In the 1960s Holiday was one of a number of gifted amateur monster-hunters roaming the shores of the loch. Combining field-work with some erudite research, he succeeded in raising the tenor of debate concerning the monster to a new level of seriousness and credibility. *The Great Orm of Loch Ness* is a monster-hunter's compendium covering a diverse range of topics. From it we may learn the art of effective loch-watching, the evolutionary history of slugs, the

---

F. W. Holiday, *The Great Orm of Loch Ness* (1968), is out of print but we can obtain second-hand copies.

legend of the Lambton Worm, aspects of Hittite folklore and the limitations of late 1960s echo-sounding technology.

The subtitle of Holiday's book is *A Practical Inquiry into the Nature and Habits of Water-Monsters*. Clearly he is no sceptic. He frequently lambasts the scientific establishment for failing to visit the loch and look into the matter. Unfortunately, the circus surrounding Nessie made it difficult for any scientist of standing to get involved and maintain their reputation. I have a collection of Loch Ness Monster postcards, and while some of them are reproductions of famous photographs, the majority are comic in tone, depicting Nessie swimming past Urquhart Castle wearing a tartan bonnet, or looking disgruntled as she is led captive through the streets of Inverness.

To counteract this tendency to levity Holiday referred to the creature as an Orm. He felt the term 'monster' had put off professional zoologists from the start. A Great Orm, he tells us, is an old Scandinavian term for a sea-serpent. This fitted in well with his theory that the creature was a species of giant worm to be found in freshwater lakes and seas across the world. He considered the Orm to be our largest indigenous creature and worthy of a lifetime of study. This is not to say that Holiday's own feelings about the monster were scientifically detached and objective: for him the creature was 'nature's ultimate horror', the very stuff of nightmares.

Loch Ness is an impressive body of water. It's 23 miles long, averages a mile in width, and has a depth of up to 1,000 feet, making it the largest of all Scottish lochs in terms of water volume (Loch Lomond has a greater surface area). Odd creatures have been seen in and near Loch Ness for hundreds of years, most famously by St Columba in the sixth century, but the modern mystery really began in the 1930s when a new road opened the loch to public scrutiny. A sighting initially published in the *Inverness Courier* in 1933 made headlines across the world and marked the beginning of a stream of eye-witness reports, photographs, theories and hoaxes that continue to this day.

The most gripping passages of
Holiday's book concern his own
monster-hunting expeditions. These
are couched in the language of adventure – as epic as any journey up
the Amazon or across the snowy
peaks of Tibet. 'I entered Scotland
on August 22nd 1962,' he writes,
describing his first trip to the loch,

Looking for Nessie

where he camped out on the shore to await developments. 'As darkness settled over the Great Glen I began to realize what a strange
place I had come to.'

Holiday was one of those lone British adventurers, usually with
wartime service behind them, by nature practical but also with a
visionary streak, who were quite common in the 1960s. In the same
year that *The Great Orm of Loch Ness* was published, two other books
by men of this hardy breed also appeared – Sir Alec Rose's *My Lively
Lady*, about his lone circumnavigation of the world, and John
Hillaby's *Journey through Britain*, which recorded his solo walk from
Land's End to John o'Groats. Holiday's quest may have been rather
more esoteric, but the laconic way in which he describes his wartime
service puts him up there with the best of them – 'In 1939 I joined
the RAF and was kept busy until 1946.'

As a keen angler, he appreciated how movements of water and
tricks of light could fool the human eye. He therefore gave particular
credence to monster-sightings made by locals who knew the loch and
its ways well – fellow-anglers, estate workers, foresters and water-
bailiffs. Interviews with them are included in the book. Having had
his own sighting of the monster during his first trip he was encour-
aged to continue his investigations, and his second encounter was
shared with some locals who watched from the opposite bank.

By now he had partially joined forces with the Loch Ness Phenomena
Investigation Bureau, an organization led by another intrepid adven-

turer, David James, author of the POW escape memoir *Escaper's Progress*. This pioneering company attempted to catch the creature on film by keeping the loch under constant observation through a system of mounted camera rigs. Holiday had further sightings of the loch's most elusive resident, but the prize of a conclusive photograph eluded him and he devotes a chapter of his book to explaining why it's so difficult to capture a clear image of the monster.

We leave our author in the summer of '67, prowling the shores of the loch for up to fourteen hours a day. He was never to be fully successful in his quest but he has left us a gripping account of the early days of monster-research, and his book is a positive encouragement to those of us who can only make occasional trips to the loch. To watch a large body of water, he tells us, requires a great deal of concentration, and a fortnight's effort is about as much as anyone can put in before their attention wavers. There is sound advice here for the inexperienced but hopeful monster-hunter. Go to the loch on a clear and calm day, preferably in July or August. Tor Point would be a good place to take up position – where the waters of the loch begin to flow into the River Ness and migratory salmon lure the creature up from the depths below. And if something strange should emerge from the dark waters in front of you be sure not to scream or shout, or slam your car door, as Nessie is shy and easily frightened. Be still, keep calm, and have your camera already in hand.

The enigma of Loch Ness is something we can all enjoy. To lose a sense of its magic is to become a duller soul. A mystery solved of course is a mystery lost, but we may admire characters like F. W. Holiday in their dedicated efforts to pierce the veil. *The Great Orm of Loch Ness* stands as testimony to one man's pursuit of the fabulous.

DAVID FLEMING has encountered many Highland monsters on his travels but only of the insect variety.

An Uneasy Peace

ANNE BOSTON

The World My Wilderness strikes me as an instance of fiction that reveals as much about time and place as bald historical facts. The novel is set in 1946, when countries, societies and most of all individuals are forced to adjust from a state of total war to an uneasy peace. Treachery, betrayal, death have cast long shadows; families or couples separated for years meet across chasms of national and personal difference. Morals are twisted and corrupted; everyone is compromised by their character, circumstances and reactions to where they find themselves, which is rarely where they thought they were. The narrative is dark, complex and subtle, with much crucial information implied obliquely or imparted as it were off-screen.

I came to this late novel by Rose Macaulay via her outstanding wartime short story 'Miss Anstruther's Letters', which packs into a few pages the agonizing loss of her lover's letters in a bombing raid that will torment poor Miss Anstruther for the rest of her life. Both works of fiction bear the stamp of total authenticity in their recall of the 'war climate', as Macaulay's friend Elizabeth Bowen described it. *The World My Wilderness* was published in 1950, her first novel in nearly ten years: an exceptional silence after her inter-war record as acclaimed author of a succession of well-received satirical novels. After her final novel *The Towers of Trebizond* (1956, see *SF* no.70), which is generally considered her finest work (though I prefer *Wilderness*), her fiction became less popular as public tastes changed.

Rose Macaulay, *The World My Wilderness* (1950)
Virago · Pb · 256pp · £8.99 · ISBN 9780349010007

There are neither heroes nor out-and-out villains in this even-handed drama. The central character is Barbary, a waiflike 17-year-old loved and neglected in equal measure by her mother Helen, with whom she survived the war stranded on the Côte d'Azur during the German occupation. Helen, a worldly creature of the senses, is typically found gambling at cards or lounging in a hammock strung outside the strawberry-pink villa that belonged to her genial, beloved second husband Maurice, who 'had collaborated mildly but prosperously from 1940 to '45 and had been thereafter found drowned in the bay'.

Meanwhile Barbary and her younger stepbrother Raoul, running wild in the hinterland, have joined the fringes of the Resistance and learned the ways of sabotage and subterfuge. Since Maurice's murder, Barbary (was she involved?) has been packed off to her lawyer father Sir Gulliver and his new wife in London to learn to be civilized, together with Raoul, who will stay with relations in the city. They will travel to London with Barbary's urbane older brother Richie, visiting his mother after three years at war and returning with relief to an orderly future as a diplomat.

Postwar London is grey and mean-spirited under rationing. Barbary is bereft, homesick for the seductive Mediterranean paradise of her adored mother, whose grief for Maurice is no less for being kept well hidden; to the girl, Sir Gulliver's sporty young wife Pamela and their small son David are 'interlopers'. After mornings studying at the Slade she bunks off to meet Raoul in the devastated City of London, along with other strays – deserters, crooks, rats and rabbits surviving in the shattered wrecks of buildings engulfed by brambles and nettles, willow-herb and bracken. Barbary sets up a shelter with Raoul, painting and selling postcards to tourists and exploring the wharves and river. Their longstanding habits of pilfering and evading the Gestapo on the Côte d'Azur transfer unthinkingly to shoplifting and dodging the City police.

In Penelope Fitzgerald's masterly introduction to Virago's 1983 reprint she observes that Rose Macaulay 'liked to insist that ideas for

novels came to her as places' – she remembered scrambling after Macaulay 'as she shinned undaunted down a crater' and waved through broken windows amid the ruined jungle of the City, where much of the novel evolves. (Macaulay, a historian, was drawn to decay and dilapidation – her next book, much reprinted, was the non-fiction *Pleasure of Ruins*.) This wilderness is both surreal and specific; I was reminded of J. G. Ballard's lost cities and drowned worlds, evoked decades later.

You can still follow the route the 'children' (teenagers not yet having been invented) took from St Paul's via Cheapside, Foster Lane, across Gresham Street into Noble Street. Within the Square Mile, today's ingeniously landscaped sudden drops to lower levels (as at twelfth-century St Alphage's and the Salters' Garden) are breathtaking proof of ancient histories layered far beneath the towers of high finance. Across London Wall the little streets and squares, bomb-blasted into oblivion, were later subsumed under the vast development of the Barbican where St Giles Cripplegate, across the water from the concert halls and cafés, stands proudly restored to use.

Barbary's damaged soul is at home among the rubble and debris but not assuaged by them; guilt is gnawing at her. She is hiding something from the world and from herself. Careless of her own safety and of her father's and Pamela's disapproval, she courts risk. Sir Gulliver senses a problem but is busy; Pamela, meeting silent non-cooperation, avoids her until the summer when they are all to join Gulliver's brother-in-law's family on their Scottish estate for a season of shooting and fishing. Barbary is fitted for a tweed suit: '"I don't suppose you shoot, do you?" Pamela said. That's all you know, Barbary . . . silently said. I don't suppose, she added to herself, you've ever sniped at Gestapo in forests. I bet you've no Gestapo suit.' Once in Scotland, she is sulky with her cousins, catapults the gamekeeper, steals money from her hostess's desk and hitchhikes back to London to avoid her psychiatrist uncle's sympathetic probing.

Sir Gulliver follows this parental nightmare to London; but, losing patience with her obstinate insistence that he reunite with her mother (we can infer he is still in love with Helen), he returns to Scotland, leaving Barbary to her dubious companions among the ruins, courting disaster.

No easy solution follows. All are capable of behaving appallingly yet remain sympathetic. When crisis forces Helen to descend on her former husband's house with her young son by Maurice, the ensuing scenes between the flinty, controlled father and the painfully jealous second wife are compassionately observed – she is 'so dull', Pamela realizes, aghast, compared with Helen, 'the courtesan now come up out of the south like a ship in full sail, singing her siren song'. Both parents concede blame for neglecting their child. Helen, who when married to Sir Gulliver had cut his dinner parties if they bored her and gone out to gamble, freely admits she has 'no conscience of any kind . . . it seems to have been left out of me'. But she is not without feeling and, realizing that her love for Barbary is unconditional whatever her daughter has done, she will use every weapon to reclaim her.

It must be said that some significant events are so glancingly mentioned you can miss them, as I did, on a first reading; and Helen as a character is an improbably gifted amalgam of artist, latter-day Georgiana at the gaming table, and even scholarly forger. But these are minor quibbles. The ending is suitably unresolved. Here is no triumphalist postwar denouement but a dishonest world where everyone (except Sir Gulliver) smuggles goods through customs and cheats on petrol and clothes rations; in the enchanting French village of Collioure, murder happens. Personal grievance is reinforced by festering animosity between the French (to the unoccupied British, corrupt collaborators) and the British (who, according to the French, ran away from the Boches in 1940). Yet a hint of redemption is to be found in love. The nearest we get to closure is in the final scene when Richie, tramping through the wrecked City, sickened by 'the squalor of ruin', takes 'the track across the wilderness towards St Paul's'.

Rose Macaulay was 67 when she wrote this atypical work. Her public face was of a clever, donnish writer, broadcaster and critic: lifelong singleton, wild swimmer, thin, rangy, much travelled, friend to many. Her family background of academics and clergymen and women 'of intelligence and conscience' was conventional enough, but not her childhood. Her mother's ill health and exhaustion from coping with six small children led the family to decamp to a fishing village near Genoa, where living was cheap and the climate gentle. The home-schooled tribe lived in and out of the sea, 'passionate and ecstatic, like a wilderness of monkeys', Macaulay remembered. Emily Rose, the second child, saw herself as a boy – as her parents had hoped – until their return to late Victorian England, shoes and stockings and Oxford High School for Girls, for which the 13-year-old, dreaming of a sailor's life, found herself hopelessly unsuited. Thanks to a benevolent uncle she went on to study at Somerville College, Oxford; thereafter her writing developed, along with hard-won independence in London from her mother after her father's death.

An admired conversationalist, Macaulay was also deeply reticent. The 1940s brought heavy loss and grief which remained mostly hidden. In 1939 Gerald O'Donovan, the married man and former priest she had loved for twenty years, was seriously injured in a car accident while she was driving and lay unconscious for many days. As an ambulance driver during the Blitz she saw terrible injury and loss of life. Her favourite sister Margaret died in early 1941. In May 1942 her flat and all her possessions were destroyed in a night of terrible bombing. The following month O'Donovan died from cancer after lingering illness. Haunted by guilt and remorse for the hurt done to Gerald's wife, Macaulay turned to the Anglo-Catholic Church of her childhood. At the same time, she could not regret their relationship (did it remain illicit partly because she preferred her unfettered life as a single woman, free to travel and maintain herself?). Their long-standing commitment to each other became public only after her death in 1958.

The postwar atmosphere in this late novel is flawlessly evoked, while the cinematic scene-setting and perceptive tracing of the traumatic buried effects of guilt and grief are surprisingly modern. Here is a fine writer operating at full stretch, well capable of exploiting and transforming the grievous insights of personal tragedy into art. In *The World My Wilderness* hidden strands of love and loss, jealousy and remorse, shaken to the surface, are traced like layers of the city's past blasted open to the world, to reveal another sort of war damage that is harder to repair.

ANNE BOSTON's anthology *Wave Me Goodbye: Stories of the Second World War* has been reissued as a Virago Modern Classic. Her biography *Lesley Blanch: Inner Landscapes, Wilder Shores* is still in print.

A Martyr to the Truth

TIM BLANCHARD

I was back home for Christmas and convalescing from the toxic fuzz induced by months of a student existence. I lay in bed mostly trying to ignore *Anna Karenina*, a brick of a Penguin Classic that I had to read before rejoining the fray. A scan of the first page had been enough to convince me Tolstoy was going to be boring. No kind of style. Ordinary plot and ideas. The work of a literary oaf who handled language like a peasant feeding chickens from his bucket.

But in the fug of the festive season the novel began to prompt the sensations that must come from wild swimming, an unexpected ease and familiarity in what had looked to be murky and unpromising waters. A clearing of the mind. A feeling that the pleasures of the novel could be endless. *Anna Karenina* was somehow, in some mysterious way, an immersion in life at its sweetest and most meaningful.

Leo Tolstoy became my first bookish passion. Not a fling – I was going to be a pale-faced acolyte. The following summer, lying on a grubby blanket in our student garden, I consumed A. N. Wilson's excellent biography in a single day. Then I walked the streets of the nearest city in holy pursuit of second-hand bookshops and lesser-known works, critical studies and commentaries, trying to discover what gives Tolstoy's novels their magical reality.

The unpredictability of book-hunting prior to the digital age meant that the one book I didn't come across was Henri Troyat's *Tolstoy* (1965). It was only twenty years later that this wonderfully

Henri Troyat, *Tolstoy* (1965), is out of print but we can obtain second-hand copies.

readable biography (still managing to seem short at almost 1,000 pages) brought it all back to me – the same questioning of the sanity of our stressful and dissatisfied civilization: wouldn't it be better to wake up with the dawn, work long days in hot fields and return in the evening for a reviving glass of fermented mare's milk?

Troyat was himself a Russian. Born Lev Aslanovich Tarassov in 1911, he had his own memories of the grotesque contrasts of Tsarist Moscow, how the velvet-upholstered interiors lit by the steady pulse of gaslight opened directly on to an abyss of poverty. In 1920, when it became clear that the Bolsheviks had prevailed, the Tarassovs fled to Constantinople before finally settling in Paris. Adopting a Gallic nom de plume, Troyat began to introduce a wider French audience of readers to the special qualities of Russian literature, writing biographies of Pushkin, Gogol, Chekhov and Dostoevsky, as well as long cycles of his own novels and short stories.

It's not surprising that Troyat managed to produce a biography of Tolstoy that is as engaging as any novel. The plot could be by Dostoevsky – a nightmarish addiction to gambling; wild nights among the gypsies; a desperate plunge into religion as an escape from despair; how Tolstoy turns his back on aristocratic privilege to wed himself to the 'dark ones', the drifters, as well as some calculating and aspirational seekers after spiritual enlightenment.

Troyat begins with a very Russian idyll. He is especially good at taking you behind the scenes of the Tolstoys' country estate of Yasnaya Polyana. The gentry did not occupy a separate, cleaned-up space away from the peasantry – as would have been the case in England – but enjoyed lives richly embroidered with the folk rituals and tastes of the muzhiks.

> In the afternoon, when the weather was fine, there were outings in the carriage with the aunts and the tutor . . . The canopied charabanc with its leather apron and the high-springed yellow cabriolet bounced along the rutted paths of the forest of Zakaz

in single file. The children shouted and sang, the horses flicked their ears. At the end of the road Matryona the cowgirl was waiting for them with black bread, sour cream and raw milk.

The heart of this epic tale, the knotted centre to all the drama that follows, is Tolstoy's courtship of his wife-to-be, Sonya. Even though we know the outcome, it is still painful to see the faltering progress of our hero towards marriage. He's like a troglodyte in full-dress uniform in the salons of Moscow and St Petersburg. Awkward and blurting. Rouble-less from losing at cards. Unable to keep his hands off the peasant girls and tortured by constant lapses from his strict 'rules of life'. A hugely promising writer who was never convinced of the value of artistic creation ('Art is a lie, and already I am no longer able to love a beautiful lie.'). A thirty-something who'd lost all his teeth, Tolstoy saw himself as old, ugly and depraved. Not much of a catch for an innocent 17-year-old girl. Beauty and the Beast with no chance of turning the Beast back into a prince.

But we know the primary reason for Tolstoy's rude exterior is a fatal yearning for truth and beauty. Inside the bear is the soul of a butterfly. His favourite piece of poetry was from Fyodor Tyutchev: 'Be quiet, lie low and hide/ Your feelings and your dreams.' The melodies of Chopin and Beethoven would bring tears to his eyes. He'd cry when he heard peasant children swearing at each other. Arguments upset him deeply. It was this combination of a bullish approach to life with a torrid sensitivity that made Tolstoy's novels miraculous.

For novelists hoping to find out how Tolstoy managed to pull it off, Troyat offers many clues. There are Tolstoy's tricks, like abandoning a conventional style in order to be clear and precise; sticking to direct, un-literary adjectives ('I never saw lips of coral, but I have seen them the colour of brick'); his way of making people stick in his readers' imagination by referring to one or two telling details, a dry pair of hands, the crease in the back of someone's neck ('a button half-undone may explain a whole side of a person's character'); not having a fixed plot in mind but allowing his characters the freedom to surprise him; and the way in which he warmed himself up by reading Dickens. Also important was Tolstoy's monstrous capacity for the research needed to ensure that every detail was based on documented reality. The lack of style wasn't the product of speedy composition. 'The margins of his drafts', observes Troyat, 'are full of trial adjectives, as a painter mixes trial colours on the edge of his palette.'

Another feature of Tolstoy's mighty engine as a novelist, I think, is his radical sincerity. He believes life has a solemn beauty. To show us what he means he dissects the hypocrisy, the artificial thinking and the behaviour of conventional society, the careful, self-aware pleasantries and the ambitions they hide. We see how the pretensions of smart, civilized society are just wallpaper. Beneath is a reality that has always something lovely and limpid about it, a truth that the most simple, uneducated and uncivilized people know.

Always truth. Tolstoy was a martyr to it. But in his effort to find and rationalize his way through essential truths he kept bumping into Death. The unavoidable fact of mortality led to his sometimes desperate search for consolation and a sense of purpose from religion, and to a great extent it ended his career as a novelist. It also meant a sad ending to his own Russian family idyll with Sonya. As father to thirteen children, Tolstoy had been master of the revels at home. There were games of football and croquet, long winter days of sledging and ice-skating. He would also charge about the house pretending to be riding a horse and invent his own games, such as dragging the children around in a giant laundry basket, swamped under clothes so that they didn't know which room they'd come to. Yasnaya Polyana had kept its muzhik charm. When the children wanted a treat they would go to a house servant who'd dole out jam with an ancient battered spoon. 'We knew why the spoon was like that,' recalled Tolstoy's son Ilya. 'It had been thrown in the garbage pail and a sow had chewed on it.'

But the Great Author turned Great Prophet could no longer bear the itch of compromise. Why was he being made to live in luxury, waited on by servants in white gloves, while all he wanted to do was put the Gospels into practice and finally plunge himself into the freshest source of peasant wisdom? Yasnaya Polyana, the Bright Glade, became a place of intrigue and misery.

Sonya could see where her husband's philosophy was heading. He would give away his writings and the estate, and the family would be left with nothing. After years of childbirth and managing the house-hold, and endless days writing up manuscripts, she at least deserved some security, to be remembered as the faithful wife of a world-renowned figure. She knew that Tolstoy's closest friend and chief advocate of Tolstoyan values, Vladimir Chertkov, had his own agenda. The sight of the man, always so mild and reasonable, gliding about her house and engaged in yet another confidential conversation with her husband drove her to mental collapse. That smooth villain Chertkov was going to take control of Tolstoy's whole body of work, including the diary containing his most intimate thoughts.

She was right to worry. At one stage, when the battle over the ownership of Tolstoy's diaries had become farcical (members of the family would try and pinch pages when no one was looking), Chertkov arranged a working group to write up a version of the diary with all positive references to Sonya removed.

By the conclusion of his biography, Troyat has made us feel the tragedy not only of the man himself – who found no revelations before he died, only muddle and noise – but also of the full cast of characters left behind with the legend, their own ghosts and regrets, and an empty house that had become the property of everyone and no one.

I wasn't meant to have been reading *Anna Karenina* for pleasure. An exam hall awaited me at the end of the year. It was only then, turning over the question paper and gripping my biro, that a feeling of outrage hit me. I had forty-five minutes to write about a novel I must have read three or four times already, I'd loved it so much. Was this all there was to the study of literature? I had an almost Tolstoyan urge to run off to the fields and escape the unfeeling rules of civilization.

For the moment, the freelance writer TIM BLANCHARD is sticking to 8 a.m. starts, working from a laptop and fuelled by decent cups of tea.

Ladies of Letters

ROGER HUDSON

Virginia Woolf's collections of essays, *The Common Reader*, *The Death of the Moth* and so on, reward those looking for interesting interstices within English literature. In the latter, in an essay entitled 'Reflections at Sheffield Place', I first met John Holroyd, 1st Lord Sheffield, and his daughter Maria Josepha, and found out about their friendship with Edward Gibbon. I then discovered that two volumes of letters by Maria Josepha and her family had appeared in the 1890s and that two more came out in the 1930s, edited by Nancy Mitford. Intrigued, I tracked them down and entered another world.

Lord Sheffield got his title for his heroics during the Gordon Riots in 1780, seizing hold of Lord George Gordon when he arrived outside Parliament at the head of his Protestant mob and promising to run him through if any of them entered the building. Later, leading a regiment of Militia, he defended the Bank of England when the mob attacked it. This was his high point: his brother-in-law, Lord Glenbervie, while recognizing his 'frankness and good nature', also remarked on his 'over-weening vanity' and how he mistook his 'very active, bustling temper and turn of mind . . . for genius'.

Virginia Woolf saw Gibbon's friendship with him as a case of the attraction of opposites, begun when they first met in Lausanne in the 1760s while Sheffield was on a Grand Tour. Besides, the Holroyds

---

The Girlhood of Maria Josepha Holroyd, 1776–1796 was published in 1896 and *The Early Married Life of Maria Josepha Lady Stanley* in 1899. *The Ladies of Alderley, 1841–1850* appeared in 1938, reissued in 1967, and *The Stanleys of Alderley, 1851–1865* in 1939, reissued in 1968. The latter two were edited by Nancy Mitford.

were a family on whose bosom Gibbon could recline in great comfort during his visits to England, while his host brought him up to date on politics and other developments. The Holroyds were proud of the friendship of this literary colossus and grateful for the huge improvement to the conversation when he was in their midst, though Maria Josepha also remarked on 'the Gib's' requirement to hold the floor, that he was 'a mortal enemy to anyone taking a walk', and that he insisted on a roaring fire every evening. He for his part saw how very intelligent she was, though too inclined not to suffer fools: 'Restrain some sallies of imagination, soften some energies of character,' he told her. Her father reminisced how 'Gibbon used to regret she was not a boy, saying she would maintain a contest well with Charles James Fox.'

In 1786, when she was 15, Maria described her daily routine to her aunt in Bath:

> Get up at 8, I walk from 9 to 10; we then breakfast; about 11 I play on the harpsichord or draw. 1, I translate, and 2 walk out again. 3, I generally read, and 4, we go in to dine. After dinner we play at backgammon; we drink tea at 7, and I work or play on the piano till 10, when we have our little bit of supper, and 11 we go to bed.

It sounds like a humdrum round such as might have been found in many country houses and rectories. But then one has to remember Gibbon's judgement on the quality of her letters at this time, with their 'mixture of just observation and lively imagery, the strong sense of a man expressed with the easy elegance of a female'. In 1789 Maria 'came out' into London society, but the following year a letter to her in Sussex from her father at his Downing Street house shows she was used to acting as his farm manager: 'Tell Fletcher while the roads are cool to send the oxen every second day from Stone to Forest Row; but that he should forward the cabbages and turnips as much as possible.'

In 1791 the Sheffield family went on a Continental tour, by chance arriving in Paris just as the King and Queen were brought back after their attempt to escape from France. There they witnessed the debates over whether the King should be put on trial, as well as the bizarre ceremony of the Apotheosis of Voltaire, who had been appropriated by the Revolution as its leading rational patron saint. Maria said, 'I could never have imagined such a piece of folly', describing the floats making up the procession, such as 'a plan and model of the Bastille; pieces of the Bastille, cut into the form of and painted to look like books, and old pieces of armour and cannon balls, which were found in the Bastille when it was taken and destroyed'.

Once Britain went to war with France in 1793, Sheffield Place became a refuge for French exiles, while on the Sussex Downs facing the Channel a series of military encampments were established in case of invasion. Among the soldiery were the Cheshire Militia and among its officers was John Thomas Stanley of Alderley, son and heir of a baronet and six years older than Maria. While she read Mary Wollstonecraft's 'many sensible and just observations' in her *Vindication* and tried to relieve some of the miseries of the poor when 'cottage visiting', Stanley became an increasing preoccupation, together with her duties as unofficial literary executor to Edward Gibbon. The historian died in 1794, leaving behind what were obviously the makings of an autobiography, and there seems every likelihood that it was Maria rather than her father whose editing enabled this classic to emerge. Stanley, whom she was to marry in 1796, had been taken out of school early to travel on the Continent with a tutor, in Neufchâtel getting to know Jane Austen's brother, Edward Knight, before mounting an expedition to Iceland in his own ship in 1789. Thereafter he was content to be the only Whig among the Cheshire gentry.

Maria's first daughter was born in 1797, to be followed with great regularity by another seven, punctuated by twin boys in 1802. Her last baby came in 1813 but she, like another boy, did not survive into adulthood. There was nothing out of the ordinary either in such a number or in the mortalities – her daughter-in-law Henrietta Maria had twelve children of whom three died as infants.

An exchange of letters with her husband Edward Stanley in 1847 seems to indicate that Henrietta tried to practise some form of contraception. When she reported that she was pregnant, he replied, 'What can you have been doing to account for so juvenile a proceeding?' She replied, 'A hot bath, a tremendous walk and a great dose have succeeded, but it is a warning.' The following year Maria Josepha is writing to her daughter-in-law about acquaintances intending 'to be delivered without knowing it', that is with the assistance of chloroform, soon to become quite acceptable after Queen Victoria took advantage of it. Anaesthetics were one of the few medical advances of these years. Maria Josepha had a leg wound 'enlivened' with caustic, while it was hoped that the new terrifying cholera could be defeated with opium pills and black pepper. As for visits to the dentist – they do not bear thinking about. The one procedure that was really successful was being 'cowpocked' against smallpox; Maria reported in 1802, 'I have had 36 children of all ages inoculated in Alderley, and all doing well.'

The Stanleys' world was one of privilege: they knew their place in the hierarchy and were content with it, since it was very near the top. They could enjoy it with the aid of numerous servants, and the new labouring masses of the north-west seldom impinged. But in January 1803 a grand dinner and entertainment, laid on for the local gentry, tenants and tradesmen to celebrate the birth of the boy twins, had to end early when 'a mob comprised of all the cotton devils in the neighbourhood began to be clamorous to get in'. They were promised two barrels of beer for themselves and diverted to a nearby bonfire and fireworks display. In 1842, at the height of the Chartist disturbances when detachments of troops and artillery had to be sent north,

the weavers go about in parties from 7 to 17 levying blackmail. The 250 who have come to our door this morning in detachments have had a small piece of bread and cheese and one horn of diluted beer, each, with which they have appeared quite satisfied . . . They professed themselves the Turned Out and not the Turnouts and all said they dare not work till the week was passed but I guess there were a few Chartists among them.

In 1843 Maria greatly enjoyed being able at no notice to go from Manchester to York to view the Minster thanks to the railway, but within weeks the family was up in arms over attempts by railway directors to get them to allow more public access to Alderley Edge. Maria remarked that the 'cottontots', meaning the mill owners and managers, 'are much more annoying to one's comfort and enjoyment than operatives as one can neither hand cuff nor great dog them if they are intrusive or offensive'. There is no mistaking Maria's Whiggery for radicalism, though she did have a soft spot for Napoleon. In March 1815 she wondered whether 'the Pope, and the Inquisition and Ferdinand, and fat Louis and his priests, and all the prejudices and bigotry of the ancient regime, which were fast returning to stultify the Continent, would be better for mankind in general than the established firm government of Napoleon', who had escaped from Elba in February.

Her hatred of Catholicism was matched by her dislike for the over-emotional approach increasingly to be found in the Church of England as a result of the Evangelical Revival. When a Stanley niece, whose father was the Bishop of Norwich, fell badly ill, Maria complained to Henrietta Maria: 'I want to hear more of the Dear Child's bodily state and less of her mental or spiritual . . . I really think you have all lost your wits – have gone into the seventh heaven of enthusiasm and forgot everything sublunary.' The tone is unmistakeably rational and Georgian, and tart too, but she could laugh at herself. When the men lingered too long over the port, she curtly demanded to know what they'd been talking about but was amused when told: 'first about the depression in the [local] salt mines, and that led us inadvertently to pepper, and that led us to cayenne, and that, my lady, led us . . . to yourself'.

She must have been daunting as a mother-in-law, for example writing to Henrietta in 1844, 'I wish I could explain to your clear understanding, that I am more annoyed sometimes by your own anxiety to keep the boys quiet . . . than by anything they can do.' But in 1845 Henrietta showed her own mettle: 'I am very glad Alice [her eldest daughter] has given satisfaction, tho' the information would have been more pleasant to me if unaccompanied by strictures on my possible conduct.'

The character traits of the mother and grandmother were present in Blanche, another of Henrietta's daughters. In 1851 Henrietta observed of her daughter's wooing: 'I do not know why he does not settle it . . . Blanche gets impatient and the more she is so the brusquer is her manner so that I really don't wonder a poor man cannot begin with sentiment.' Nancy Mitford remembered being taken, aged 4, to see Blanche, Countess of Airlie, her great-grandmother, and her reprimand when it emerged that she did not yet speak French: 'There is nothing so inferior as a gentlewoman who has no French.'

Maria's pugnacity did not fade with age. In 1853 in the preliminaries to the Crimean War she said, 'I would like to hear that the Russian fleet is annihilated on the Black Sea.' Even in 1862, the year before she died, when Britain was preparing against the possibility of being drawn into the American Civil War on the side of the Southern states, she wrote, 'I *could* be sorry that such preparations should not be used for giving those wretches a good drubbing & when I look at the map, I DO covet *Maine* so much.'

ROGER HUDSON's *An Englishman's Commonplace Book* was published by Slightly Foxed at the end of 2020. For those who would like to read more about the letters and the family, Roger has supplied an appendix which can be found on our website: see www.foxedquarterly.com/roger-hudson-ladies-of-letters.

Philosophical Designs

MARIANNE FISHER

Sometimes you come across a book that changes how you view the world. For me one such was Robert Bringhurst's *The Elements of Typographic Style* (1st ed. 1992). My father gave me a copy of the third edition when I was just beginning my own career as a copy-editor, and it opened my eyes to a new philosophy of life applied to the arrangement of type. Until then, I had never really thought about what text looked like. I liked books to have attractive covers, but the words inside were just words, weren't they? How wrong I was.

The Elements of Typographic Style is concerned with the printed word in its own right, as something more than a vehicle of meaning. Printed in black, grey and red on creamy laid paper, the book is, in Bringhurst's own words, 'the fruit of a lot of long walks in the wilderness of letters: in part a pocket field guide to the living wonders that are found there, and in part a meditation on the ecological principles, survival techniques and ethics that apply'. Which is to say that it is a book about what makes a page or a letterform 'good' (in other words, both functional and pleasing), how such things have been achieved in the past, and how one might go about achieving them today.

This balancing of the philosophical with the practical is evident even in the chapter titles: 3 Harmony and Counterpoint; 6 Choosing and Combining Type; 11 Prowling the

·ABTHEÇD
ELEMENTS
J K Ł O F U V
W T Y P O - X
G R A P H I C
Q S T Y L E Z
á à â ǎ ą̃ æ ą ä å ã
þ Robert Bringhurst ð
ø 1 2 3 4 5 6 7 8 9 0 ᴅ

A new edition of Robert Bringhurst's *The Elements of Typographic Style: Version 4.3* (2013) is available in paperback: Hartley & Marks · 382pp · £29.95 · ISBN 9780881792126.

Specimen Books. On p.78, in a section called 'Consider even the lowly hyphen', we read of how the first hyphens were single canted penstrokes (the narrowest stroke a pen could make), how their slopes varied with shifting human inclinations, and how Renaissance typographers could choose between the canted hyphen and the flat hyphen. Some preferred one, some the other, and some 'mixed the two at random . . . to give a touch of scribal variety to the typeset page'. On p.79 we are in more practical territory: 'If you are tempted to re-design an existing font, using a digital font editor, the hyphen is a good character to start on.'

That 'scribal variety to the typeset page' is telling, for this book is deeply humane and humanist. In the foreword Bringhurst points out that, for as long as people have been writing, the principles of the good page have been based 'on the structure and scale of the human body – in particular the eye, the hand and the forearm – and on the invisible but no less real, no less demanding and no less sensual anatomy of the human mind'. That underlying humanity never dies: even the most technical discussion of mathematical proportions matters only in so far as it will help to produce that which is pleasing to human eyes, hands and minds. The writing itself is likewise a joy: witty, clear and striking. Bringhurst (who is poet and translator as well as prose writer and typographer) has a genuine flair for metaphor and writes with the forthright confidence of one who trusts his readers to be interested or be gone.

And interested you must surely be. Here you will explore the history and spirit of different fonts, and the associations they bring with them; you will learn about page proportions and how they may be related to the mathematics of the eight-note musical scale; about text figures and lining figures, small caps and titling faces, and how best to use them; how to distinguish true italic from sloped roman. You will gather printers' flowers; you will discover the beauty of empty space.

A book about typography had better be an example in itself, and *The Elements of Typographic Style* is just that. An unusual shape –

about twice as tall as it is wide – it sits comfortably in the hand and will surprise and delight you with every lively, lyrical page. It shows while it tells: when you are advised to do X instead of Y, both X and Y are illustrated so you can see the difference for yourself; a discussion of outdenting is set in outdented paragraphs so you can grasp its effect; margins are put to surprising uses. Extracts from Plato, Aristotle, the Song of Songs, Thoreau and Dostoevsky are set to provide typographical examples. (Bringhurst himself is Canadian, but his outlook here is global: Arabic, Asian and Russian scripts feature in the discussion as well as Latin and Greek.) After each reading you will come away not only more knowledgeable, but also refreshed by having interacted with a lovely and stimulating thing, in the company of a human being so generous as to lavish attention on an apostrophe.

Such generosity is perhaps not altogether practical. 'The first task of the typographer is . . . to read and understand the text; the second task is to analyse and map it.' Few typographers today, I fear, can afford themselves the luxury of actually *reading* the texts they set. 'Give full typographical attention even to incidental details.' How many publishing schedules allow that? But the philosophy holds true nonetheless, for the ability to imagine and aspire to the seemingly unattainable is surely one of humankind's more admirable traits. And in any case, this model of best practice is not to be followed uncritically: typography 'should honour the text for its own sake – always assuming that the text is worth a typographer's trouble'. Bad text does not deserve good letters. Such profound respect for one's craft and its tools – and, indeed, for oneself as craftsman – is both humbling and exciting.

But why should any of this matter? Is it not merely what my friends are pleased to call 'font fetishism'? Does all this talk of kerning and the Golden Section not reek of pretension? I don't think so. For although typography considers written words as aesthetic entities in their own right, it does not forget that they are first and foremost the servants of sense. The ultimate purpose of typography is to make reading as pleasant as might be, sparing the reader discomfort and distraction, and thereby freeing that reader's energy and intellect to attend to what the words *mean*. Good typography is the glass lamp that shields the candle of civilization, that its light may shine through steady and clear.

MARIANNE FISHER enjoys hunting good typography in the wilderness of letters and tries to remain philosophical.

The Crème de la Crème

CHRISTOPHER RUSH

Muriel Spark's most famous novel was published in 1961. It is set in 1930s Edinburgh, and the characters include schoolgirls at Marcia Blaine's High School for Girls, the dull headmistress Miss Mackay, the singing teacher, the art master and, of course, the unforgettable Miss Brodie, the mainspring of the action. The so-called Brodie set of girls are what she calls the *crème de la crème*, the elite, the elect, the chosen few, chosen by Miss Brodie herself, their presiding deity.

The novel opens in 1936 when the girls are 16, flashes back to 1930 when they are in the Junior School, in Miss Brodie's sole charge, and ends in 1938, with a final flash forward to the unexpected death of Miss Brodie, aged 56, in 1946: a span of sixteen years. At the start the flamboyantly dogmatic Miss Brodie, having reached the age of 39, is in her prime, as she puts it, and has chosen to share it with those chosen few, specifically six girls of her set: Monica Douglas, Rose Stanley, Eunice Gardner, Sandy Stranger, Jenny Gray and Mary Macgregor. A seventh and late arrival is Joyce Emily Hammond.

Miss Brodie herself is a mass of contradictions. She distrusts the Catholic Church and the school's team-spirit, exemplified by the Girl Guides, but adores Italian religious art and admires Mussolini and his fascists. She proclaims the glory of passionate romantic love but rejects her own true love, the art master Teddy Lloyd, because he's a married man and a Catholic, and settles for a more subdued affair with the singing teacher, the respectably dreary Gordon Lowther.

Muriel Spark, *The Prime of Miss Jean Brodie* (1961)
Penguin · Pb · 144pp · £8.99 · ISBN 9780141181424

She is also rigidly dogmatic: although she professes to be an inspiring bringer-out of her charges' innate abilities, as opposed to a mere mechanical putter-in of facts and principles, she rides rough-shod over the girls' minds, and brooks no opposition to her ideas and her whims. Sandy sees this eventually, understanding that the girls of her set are mere surrogates whose purpose is to satisfy their teacher's frustrations. Finally she betrays her to the headmistress, revealing that she has taught fascism and influenced the last of her set, Joyce Emily, to go and fight for Franco in Spain, where she is subsequently killed.

In later life Sandy converts to Roman Catholicism, writes a treatise entitled *The Transfiguration of the Commonplace*, which brings her fame, and withdraws from the world to become a nun, Sister Helen of the Transfiguration. When asked by a visitor what has been the primary influence on her, she grips the bars of her grille desperately and answers quite simply, 'There was a Miss Jean Brodie in her prime.' A great teacher may not always get it right, may even hopelessly distort and mislead. But in the end such a teacher does transform the commonplace and, like art itself, heightens experience. These teachers never leave us. We are always in their classrooms.

That is partly what the novel is about. But it's also about many other things.

It's about sex, seen through the eyes of schoolgirls. Miss Brodie plays on their sexual awareness and this provides some of the hilarity, when they imagine her having sex with Mr Lowther on the top of Arthur's Seat in a howling storm – a banal bed would not be good enough for Miss Brodie; and in the concocted correspondence between the two teachers, written by Sandy and Jenny, the last letter in the series ending with Miss Brodie's final flourish: 'Allow me, in conclusion, to congratulate you warmly upon your sexual intercourse, as well as your singing!' You can just hear Miss Brodie's formal accents beneath the girls' immature fantasies.

More seriously, it's about betrayal. The teacher is the prophet, the girls are her disciples, and one of them betrays her. When Peter faced up to his betrayal of Jesus he went out and wept. Judas went out and hanged himself. Sandy withdraws from the world but does not find peace as a nun. Her betrayed teacher haunts her from the grave.

It's about religion, too, specifically about the Calvinism on which Muriel Spark herself turned her back when she left Presbyterian Edinburgh and converted to Catholicism. The Brodie set are the elect, and their teacher is free to direct their fates as she sees fit. It's about manipulation and control by an unchallengeable idol – except it doesn't work out for her that way.

It's about duality, the theme of double identity or split personality reinforced by the Edinburgh setting, the poverty and decay of the Old Town and the wealthy respectability of the New Town, which hadn't changed much since the death of Robert Louis Stevenson – think of his Dr Jekyll – only three decades earlier. The city is therefore the perfect setting for the dangerously divided Miss Brodie, whose ancestor, Deacon Brodie, also led a double life, town councillor by day and criminal by night. He too came to a sticky end, hanged on a gallows of his own devising. So it's also about incongruities, and about the nasty surprises God has in store for you. And the split mentality rubs off on Sandy, who leads a double life of her own, sleeping with Teddy Lloyd while entering into imaginary relationships with fictitious figures such as Stevenson's Alan Breck, Charlotte Brontë's Mr Rochester and others, including the Lady of Shalott, deliberately used by the author as a frustrated figure who sees life not directly but through a mirror, and weaves her own version of reality into a tapestry. As soon as she does encounter reality she is destroyed. Sandy's identification with this doomed figure foreshadows her future existence as a nun, embowered by four grey walls and four grey towers. The difference is that Sandy understands what is happening to her, whereas Miss Brodie remains divided and deluded.

But above all else it's about Sandy's transformation of the commonplace, which she has learnt from her teacher, flawed though she is. This takes me back to the end of the 1960s, when I enrolled at an Edinburgh teacher-training college. It was a staid establishment, but one moment stood out, when a young lecturer announced to us: 'Teaching is a branch of show business!' I never forgot those words, and went on to smuggle through instruction in the guise of entertainment, performing antics for which nowadays I'd be locked up: leaping from a cupboard to stab Claudius (a Sixth Form boy) with a blackboard pointer; passing round glasses of claret to let the class taste Keats's draught of vintage; not to mention declaiming Gray's *Elegy* in Edinburgh graveyards with the pupils recumbent on table-top tombstones – which were probably unsafe. All no longer possible, not today, not since schools became bureaucratized, and teaching became an education industry where individuality is unsafe.

Still, I feel there should be room for the Miss Brodies of this world. We need teachers who can turn the commonplace into magic. My daughter Jenny, reading English at Edinburgh University, recently wrote a comparative essay on *The Prime of Miss Jean Brodie* and *The Tempest*. The classroom is the island. Miss Brodie is Prospero, the all-powerful magician, the controller, masterminding and manipulating her pupils. Prospero has also been betrayed but like Miss Brodie he can still put on a great show – the cloud-capped towers, the gorgeous palaces, the solemn temples, 'a most majestic vision', even as it dissolves and melts into thin air, just as with Miss Brodie whose name and memory after her death 'flitted from mouth to mouth like swallows in summer, and in winter they were gone'.

In his Epilogue, Prospero tells the audience that his project or purpose has been *to please*, in other words to entertain. The educator who fails to teach Caliban nevertheless bows out as the entertainer, the wizard who transfigures the trite and makes the mundane marvellous. As Miss Brodie surely knew, teaching is indeed a branch of show business.

CHRISTOPHER RUSH was a teacher in Edinburgh for thirty years. He is now a writer, and still in his prime.

A Nasty Business

ADAM SISMAN

H. G. Wells's *The War of the Worlds* (1897) has long been one of my favourite books. I first read it half a century ago – when I was about 10, to judge by the date on my Penguin edition (price 3/6d). I must have read it half a dozen times since; my battered copy is now held together with Sellotape. Recently I began watching a television adaptation: it was so disappointing that I abandoned it halfway through the first episode. This unhappy experience led me to question why it is that I like the book so much.

The most obvious reason is that it is a compelling story. From the famous opening paragraph, which imagines aliens studying mankind across the abyss of space, rather as humans might contemplate infusoria under a microscope, our attention is seized; and it remains gripped through to the end.

The action of the novel is set in the last years of the nineteenth century, and is told in retrospect, looking back on the Martian invasion six years before. The story is narrated in the first person, which gives it the immediacy of an eye-witness report. The narrator is a writer 'on philosophical themes', a modern man of science, much like Wells himself. He addresses us as kindred spirits. 'The planet Mars, I scarcely need remind the reader, revolves about the sun at a mean distance of 140,000,000 miles . . .' He refers to 'men like Schiaparelli' and 'Perrotin of Nice' as if these astronomers would be familiar to us.

H. G. Wells, *The War of the Worlds* (1897)
Penguin · Pb · 240pp · £6.99 · ISBN 9780141441030

The narrator lives on the edge of Woking, about twenty-five miles south-west of London – as Wells was doing at the time; indeed the house that he lived in is still standing, now graced with a blue plaque. One characteristic of the novel is the strong sense of place, reinforced by frequent references to the satellite towns and suburbs – Weybridge, Walton-on-Thames, Shepperton, Hampton, Richmond, Kew, Sheen and so on – through which the narrator passes as he flees from the Martian advance. Apparently Wells researched his locations on a bicycle.

The entire novel takes place in and around London. The reader never learns whether Martians have landed elsewhere. There is some logic to this, given that Britain was then the predominant power of the age, the centre of an apparently mighty empire that covered a quarter of the surface of the globe. London could still be described as 'the Mother of all Cities'. It was, then, an obvious place for an alien attack. But in any case, the reader does not care what has happened elsewhere; with only a minor intermission, we are with the narrator throughout, sharing his fears and privations.

The world that Wells describes is not so different from the one we know today. Many of the local residents commute into the city by train; in the evenings they return to relax, perhaps taking a leisurely bicycle ride or a stroll in the pine-woods, or chatting to their neighbours over the garden wall; at the weekend they play golf or go boating on the river. Science has tamed nature and made life comfortable. There is no television, but there are both morning and evening newspapers; no telephone, but a very efficient postal service, and telegrams for urgent communication. Milk is delivered by cart to the house each morning. With hindsight the unnamed narrator remarks on the complacency of that time, innocent of the coming catastrophe. 'It seemed so safe and tranquil.'

It is this very familiarity, this sense of everything being normal and peaceful, that makes the subsequent chaos and destruction so shocking.

The narrator is one of the first to catch sight of a Martian, having come across a huge smoking cylinder, about thirty yards in diameter, almost buried where it has crash-landed in sandy heathland near his house. Later other cylinders land nearby. At this stage there is little sense of danger. The arrival of the cylinder attracts more curiosity than apprehension; a small crowd gathers, and only when the cylinder opens and a Martian is seen does alarm ensue. 'Those who have never seen a living Martian can scarcely imagine the strange horror of its appearance . . . Even at this first encounter, this first glimpse, I was overcome with disgust and dread.'

The Martians are oblivious to a deputation of learned men trying to establish communication. They sweep the area around the cylinder with a heat-ray, bringing instant death to anyone within range. The narrator is lucky to escape with his life. But even then there is no widespread panic. The Martians, though hideous and evidently hostile, are bulky creatures, capable only of laboured movements in earth's greater gravity; it seems obvious that they cannot leave the vicinity of their landing-site, and should they pose a continuing threat, they will quickly be destroyed. Soldiers are already moving into position around the site. The narrator returns home to supper with his wife, confident that the authorities will soon have the situation under control.

The next day is hot and sultry; a thunderstorm is brewing. Feeling uneasy, the narrator hires a dogcart to take his wife to the safety of Leatherhead, ten miles distant, before returning at night. On the ride back the weather breaks. Amid thunderclaps and lightning flashes, he glimpses, through the lashing rain, a nightmare vision:

a monstrous tripod, higher than many houses, striding over the young pine trees, and smashing them aside in its career; a walking engine of glittering metal, striding now across the heather; articulate ropes of steel dangling from it, and the clattering tumult of its passage mingling with the riot of the thunder.

This is his first sight of a Martian fighting machine. He cowers in the mud until it has passed; once again he is lucky to have escaped. With their superior technology the invaders are quickly able to crush any resistance. In the next few days the Martians will advance on London, sweeping the ground with heat-rays and laying down clouds of poisonous gas to smother the artillerymen 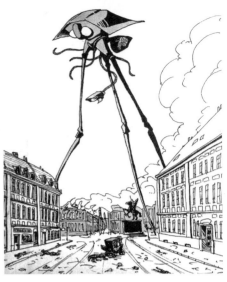 who have been positioned to protect the capital. The war of the worlds is not much of a war: it is a massacre. Only when humanity is helpless and civilization on the brink of collapse do the Martians succumb to an unforeseen enemy.

In his flight from the advancing Martians, the narrator is caught on the bank of the Thames where it meets the Wey and survives only by flinging himself into the river. When he emerges, the charred bodies and ruined buildings all around remind him of images of Pompeii.

At this point in the story Wells skilfully switches perspective, to that of the narrator's brother, a medical student in London. Thus he is able to describe the terror and confusion in the city from the point of view of someone who was there. As the Martians approach from the south-west, a mass exodus begins. Fearful Londoners flee northwards and eastwards, jostling and trampling each other in their desperation. The veneer of civilization is torn aside: a cart is driven over a man's back; men try to drag women from their carriage; a train ploughs through a crowd. With difficulty the narrator's brother reaches the Essex coast: there, by paying an extortionate fare, he succeeds in securing a place aboard a paddle-steamer bound for Ostend. As this moves slowly out to sea amid a mass of other vessels, Martian fighting machines appear on the shore – and then begin wading out in their pursuit. He witnesses one of the few victories for mankind when a naval vessel, *The Thunder-Child*, rams one of the Martian machines and destroys it, before itself exploding under the glare of the heat-ray.

Meanwhile the narrator is trapped in a ruined house in Mortlake, with Martians encamped outside. He is confined there for fifteen days, hungry and thirsty, witnessing through a spyhole in the rubble the grisly fate of human captives of the Martians. The claustrophobia and dread of this period of incarceration are powerfully evoked. Imprisoned with him in the ruined house is a curate, whose grip on reality, already loosened by the catastrophe, gradually fails. On the eighth day the curate begins crying out to his Maker in woe, attracting the attention of the Martians outside – until he is silenced by a blow. His body is dragged away by their probing tentacles. Eventually, the narrator emerges, to find the Martians gone. 'And oh! The sweetness of the air!'

Dazed, he wanders through the desolate and silent suburbs of Putney and Wimbledon, the only signs of life being the occasional stray dog or the odd furtive figure scurrying for shelter like a disturbed scavenging rodent. Eventually he arrives in the centre of the city, to see the dome of St Paul's with a great gash in its side. He remains fearful of the absent Martians, until he comes across a fighting machine on the summit of Primrose Hill and sees 'a multitude of black birds circling and clustering about the hood', picking at the decaying body of the Martian inside.

The War of the Worlds, first published in serial form in 1897, was one of a cluster of novels that established Wells's reputation as the 'father of science fiction', following *The Time Machine* (1895) and *The Island of Dr Moreau* (1896: see *SF* no.66), and *The Invisible Man*, also published in 1897. One can detect its influence on many subsequent novels, by writers as diverse as John Wyndham and J. G. Ballard. *The War of the Worlds* also satisfied the appetite for 'invasion literature', then growing keener as the perception of the danger from Germany grew. The most notable exponent of this genre was William Le Queux, whose invasion novel *The Great War in England in 1897* was published in the same year. In *The War of the Worlds* Wells makes a passing reference to the German threat when he remarks that the arrival of the first Martian cylinder 'certainly did not make the sensation an ultimatum to Germany would have done'.

One can consider the novel as a parable of colonialism. Wells later revealed that the plot of *The War of the Worlds* had been inspired by reading about the slaughter of the indigenous people of Tasmania. In the text itself the narrator draws this parallel:

And before we judge of them too harshly, we must remember what ruthless and utter destruction our own species has wrought, not only upon animals, such as the vanished bison and the dodo, but upon its own inferior races. The Tasmanians, in spite of their human likeness, were entirely swept out of existence in a war of extermination waged by European immigrants, in the space of fifty years. Are we such apostles of mercy as to complain if the Martians warred in the same spirit?

Perhaps this gives *The War of the Worlds* a contemporary currency – if we ignore the jarring reference to 'inferior races'. The TV adaptation tried to make the book relevant to twenty-first century concerns, and thereby diluted much of the period flavour that makes the book so enjoyable. This was a mistake: the novel still works for us as it was originally written: an enthralling story, vividly told.

ADAM SISMAN is a writer, specializing in biography. His most recent book is *The Professor and the Parson: A Story of Desire, Deceit and Defrocking* (2019). You can also hear him discussing the art of biography in Episode 6 of our podcast, 'Well-Written Lives'.

Fidget Pie

SUE QUINN

Huffkins and Fleads, Surry Ponds and
Manchets, Frumenty, Minnow Tansies and
Fidget Pie. These evocative recipe titles were
what first hooked me; fantastical-sounding to my ear, they might
have sprung from the pages of a Lewis Carroll story. They were,
in fact, authentic recipes in an extraordinary volume I found in a
second-hand bookshop more than a decade ago called *Good Things
in England*, by Florence White. It wasn't *Alice in Wonderland*, but it
led me down a rabbit hole of sorts. I've been obsessed with the book
and its author ever since.

For readers unfamiliar with it, let me explain. *Good Things in
England* is a cookery book or perhaps, more precisely, a compendium
of 853 recipes, some dating from the fourteenth century, that White
collected from or traced to specific regions of England. When it was
published in 1932, *The Times* hailed it as 'one of the most romantic
cookery books ever written' and Lady Hope in the *Guardian* declared,
'No household should be without this most original cookery book.'
The public adored it too. The first edition flew off the shelves and the
publishers rushed to issue a second imprint within a couple of
months. Since then, *Good Things in England* has been a crucial source
of recipes for most other books on English cookery, while chefs, food
writers and historians have showered it with praise. Elizabeth David
was a devotee and so was Jane Grigson.

Florence White, *Good Things in England* (1932)
Persephone · Pb · 400pp · £15 · ISBN 9781903155004

As a testament to its continued relevance and undiminished charm, Persephone reissued it in 1999 (of the many editions I now own, this is the one I cook from, its splattered pages evidence of my Florence White fixation). And in 2010, the *Observer* listed *Good Things in England* in its Top 50 cookbooks ever written, pronouncing it part cookbook, part historical document and 'a lost classic'. The question is: why was it ever lost in the first place? By rights, it should be as renowned as *Mrs Beeton's Book of Household Management*.

Florence White (1863–1940) was born and raised in Peckham, London. She lost her mother when she was 6, and soon after was blinded in one eye (which ended her marriage prospects, so she was told). She worked variously as a governess, teacher, journalist, lady's companion and cook-housekeeper into her late fifties. Then, when poor health forced her to give up domestic service, she set out to become the first freelance journalist specializing in food and cookery. She wrote prolifically – her work appeared in the *Edinburgh Evening News*, *The Times*, the *Spectator*, the *Listener* and the *Lady* – and along the way she discovered her passion for traditional English cookery.

When she sat down at her typewriter in her Earls Court flat in the winter of 1931–2 to write *Good Things in England*, she was attempting a different kind of cookbook from those that had gone before. In 1927, fed up with England's reverence for French cuisine, she had set out to 'capture the charm of England's cookery before it is completely crushed out of existence'. She travelled from county to county, 'tumbling on and off trains', and approached housewives and farmers, household cooks, dairymaids and mistresses of stately homes. Essentially, she spoke to anyone from whom she could coax a recipe by, as she put it, 'stirring up their memories and inspiring them to hunt up written and printed records'. She also wrote to *The Times*, appealing to readers for their own favourite old English recipes. The public responded in droves. By the end of 1928, not only had she amassed sufficient recipes for two books (the second, *Good English Food*, was published posthumously in 1952), she had also established the English Folk Cookery Association to fly the nation's culinary flag.

White was hoping to rescue England's food heritage from oblivion and to challenge the commonly held view that English food was abominable. She believed that well-executed English cookery ranked among the best in the world. By this she meant dishes prepared down the ages by proficient home cooks who lived close to the source of their food in farmsteads and country houses (although she acknowledged that English cookery was profoundly shaped by recipes, ingredients and culinary traditions from other lands, including those of Empire). She was exasperated that England had all but forgotten the delicious treasures under its own nose. *Good Things in England* would be her manifesto.

White didn't want her book to be a museum piece; she hoped readers would keep the recipes alive by cooking them, as evidenced by its subtitle, *A Practical Cookery Book for Everyday Use*. She arranged the chapters in an orderly manner, dividing them into courses and sub-courses, and devoted a section to particularly wonderful regional and national specialties. She also included an index, invaluable for the home cook.

The following recipe is one of my favourites. Sir Charles Bernard, Chief Commissioner of Burma, gave it to White, explaining that his wife made it for him every day for 'tiffin'. White's disdain for inferior versions is palpable in her end note.

Baked Rice Pudding
1887

Ingredients: rice 2oz; milk 1 pint; sugar 2oz; butter or finely chopped suet 1oz; nutmeg.

Time: To bake 4 hours

METHOD

1. Wash the rice.
2. Put it in the bottom of a pie dish.

3. Sprinkle the sugar over it.
4. Then the suet.
5. Pour in the milk.
6. Stir well.
7. Grate some nutmeg over the top and put the dish into a very slow oven.
8. If by any chance it looks as if it is getting too dry, add a little more milk.

NB: Properly cooked the rice and milk at the end of 4 hours are deliciously creamy, and the top a 'symphony' in delicate gold and brown. A veritable poem of a pudding. Prepared in this way, nursery children love it. It is its degenerate form that is so much disliked.

Many of the old recipes strike me as thoroughly contemporary. This one, from Charles Elmé Francatelli, chef to Queen Victoria, would be at home on any modern British restaurant menu.

Marrow Toast
1846

Ingredients: A marrow bone; boiling water; salt; pepper; chopped parsley; lemon juice; shallot, a mere suspicion; squares of hot crisp toast.

Time: Sufficient to make the toast, chop the parsley and cook the marrow for a minute.

METHOD

1. Get the butcher to break the marrow bone.
2. Cut the marrow into small pieces the size of a filbert.
3. Just parboil them in boiling water with a little salt for one minute.

4. Drain instantly upon a sieve, keep hot.
5. Season with a little chopped parsley, pepper and salt, lemon juice and a mere suspicion of finely chopped shallot.
6. Toss lightly altogether, spread it out upon squares of hot crisp dry toast, and serve immediately.

And the following confections are so utterly delicious I make them often, using ready-ground almonds as a shortcut.

Almond Puffs
1769

Ingredients: sweet almonds 2oz; orange flower water; eggs, the whites of 3; caster sugar 6oz.

Time: About 1 hour or longer in a very cool oven, till a delicate brown and crisp.

METHOD

1. Prepare a flat baking sheet, brush it over with oiled butter and when that is cold and set dredge it with flour; give it a knock to distribute the flour and shake out any that may be loose.
2. Blanch the almonds, and pound them fine in a stone mortar with some orange flower water.
3. Beat the whites of the eggs to a very stiff froth (quite dry).
4. Add about one ounce of sugar, folding it in from the side so as not to break the egg froth.
5. Add the pounded almonds in the same way.
6. Then fold in the rest of the sugar.
7. Lay it in dessertspoonfuls in little round cakes on the tin and bake as directed.

But *Good Things in England* is more than just a volume of recipes. White was a gifted social historian and an accomplished writer. She whisks you away on a journey that traverses England and crosses the social divide, stopping at farmhouses and rectories, royal castles and stately homes, grand hotels and domestic kitchens. And she has you yearning one minute for buns slicked with golden syrup and cream, as scoffed by schoolboys in Devon, the next for roast chicken with prunes sizzling in the oven of a Lancashire farmhouse. A recipe for bilberry pies evokes the Yorkshire parsonage where the Brontë sisters enjoyed them for tea, while a tart of artichoke bottoms conjures the days of Queen Anne.

For me, recipes from the general public are the real treasures. White refrains from editing their words, so allowing us to hear their voices, and this imbues the dishes with extra flavour. Of a Sheep's Trotters recipe, a Bolton lady writes: 'We eat sheep's trotters boiled in Bolton, it is a sort of ritual. When the Football Wanderers bring home the Cup, they are received with sheep's trotters decorated with white and blue ribbons.' Or of a Fish Roll recipe, Miss Cullen from Leamington, Warwickshire, explains: 'To be quite honest this is a wartime [1914–18] emergency dish for a meatless day, but it's too good to lose.'

Like Mrs Beeton before her, White intended *Good Things in England* to be relevant for both the mistress of the house and the household cook (as well as the many women who, by this time, performed both functions). She also assumed a level of intellectual curiosity among her readers.

The book has its idiosyncrasies. White can be rather doctrinaire, adamant that the traditional method is the best and only way to cook a dish. On apple pie, for example, she writes:

A horrible plan is frequently adopted in cheap or middle-class restaurants of simply stewing some apples, baking a sheet of pastry on a tin, and serving a wedge of it on the stewed apple and calling it apple pie. This is a direct insult to the real thing, and to the customer who knows better.

Elsewhere, though, she is reflective and lyrical. She ponders:

'Think what a poem a salad might be if "dressed" with primrose vinegar.'

More than a decade after first picking up the book, I still find the recipe titles in *Good Things in England* alluring. And the temptation to cook them is irresistible, as White draws back the curtains and offers me a peek inside the kitchens of the past. Fidget Pie was the last dish I cooked. It's simply made with sliced potatoes, apple and bacon layered in a baking dish and draped in 'a rather good short crust'. Once upon a time, it was devoured by famished harvesters for supper. And it still tastes as delicious as it sounds.

SUE QUINN is a cookbook author and food writer. Her most recent book, *Cocoa: An Exploration of Chocolate*, with recipes, is published by Quadrille. She is now writing a biography of Florence White.

The illustrations in this article are by Gillian Zeiner and first appeared in Jane Grigson's *English Food* (1974).

Lest We Forget

BRAD BIGELOW

'Lost in Poland?' the publisher Heinemann asked in October 1939 in
a newspaper advertisement for Martin Hare's new novel *Polonaise*.
The last correspondence the publishers had had from the novelist,
a letter from Warsaw sent just before the outbreak of war, assured
them that 'We are perfectly calm here.' The advertisement went on:
'Nobody now knows the fate of the author of *Polonaise*.'

At that moment, neither did the author herself. As later recounted
in her memoir, *My Name Is Million* (1940), she and her husband were
at that moment huddled inside a guard post on the border between
Russian-occupied Poland and Lithuania, waiting to hear whether
they would be allowed to cross. They had been on the run for weeks.

I first came across Martin Hare as the author of the novel *Butler's
Gift*, a light comedy set in Ireland on the brink of civil war, and
assumed its author was a man. Curious to know more I began to
investigate.

To my surprise, a newspaper article from late 1934 identified
'Martin Hare' as an Irishwoman named Zoe Girling. In it she was
pictured with her husband, Aleksander Zajdler, a Polish nobleman
and former army officer whom she had married the year before. The
couple had met in Paris. She knew no Polish and he had little English,
so they communicated in French. They later moved to Poland, where
they divided their time between Warsaw and his family's estate in the
Carpathians. And there they might have lived happily ever after with

---

Anon. [Lucy Zoe Girling Zajdler, also known as Martin Hare], *My Name Is
Million* (1940), is out of print but we can obtain second-hand copies.

Zoe continuing to write clever comic novels as Martin Hare, had history not intervened.

Zoe posted the manuscript of *Polonaise*, her seventh novel, set in Poland, along with that reassuring note to her publisher, on 31 August 1939. The next day, the Germans invaded. The speed with which the Blitzkrieg rolled over the weak and ill-prepared Polish forces stunned everyone. Luftwaffe bombs began falling on Warsaw on the first day of the war, and by the next day the city was ablaze. To its residents, the advance of the Germans seemed like 'a green wall of water racing inland, in just that fraction of a second before it topples over and breaks and drowns the land'. By 4 September, Zoe and Aleksander had left Warsaw, taking with them only what they could fit into a couple of rucksacks and joining thousands of other refugees clogging the roads to the east.

If the German invasion of Poland was one of the great sweeps of history's broom, *My Name Is Million* is that history told from the dust's perspective. All the certainties of life the couple had known quickly crumbled. As petrol supplies ran out, a car became an encumbrance: you could have bought a Rolls-Royce 'for a cigarette', wrote Zoe. She and her husband avoided speaking to one another in French for fear of being taken for spies or fifth columnists, while he worried that her imperfect command of Polish might put her at risk. Money lost any value. Aleksander resorted to what his wife called his 'officer manner' to beg cart rides from peasants: 'The officer manner could always, in the end, get us out of the village and, once we had moved, obtain, say, ten kilometres where fifteen had been promised and six really intended.'

While riding in one of these carts, Zoe watched as a Heinkel bomber swept down over their column of refugees. A moment later, she was lying in a ditch, blood streaming into her eyes, her scalp sliced open by shrapnel. They managed to find a field hospital in Lublin where they persuaded a nurse to stitch it up. When they reached Chelm, they found not a town but 'a crater in hell'. Like millions of Poles, they were homeless, with 'no plan, no provisions, no idea where they were going; nowhere to go'. One of Zoe's few remaining comforts was her diary, in which she recorded her chaotic impressions: 'I was caught in a machine of whose working I had no real knowledge, battered about by the horrible ebb and flow of rumour, with all landmarks and seeming certainties underwater.' Crammed in a railway car with a hundred others, creeping cautiously towards yet another town in the hope of finding sanctuary, she came to appreciate the fine margin between comfort and discomfort: 'It may be, in fact it cannot be, more than some knack evolved of freeing an arm or a leg for an instant from the pressure of all the other arms and legs above and below it; or perhaps being nearer to what air there is, or farther from it.'

Eventually they headed for the estate of an elderly noblewoman whom they knew in the Polesian marshes near the border with Russia. They were warmly welcomed, but only a few days later they awoke to the news that Russian forces were crossing into Poland. Many Poles still remembered the Soviet occupation of eastern Poland during the 1919–21 conflict. 'The stream of refugees now began to flow in the opposite direction,' observed Zoe. And now their status became a death warrant. Zoe was a foreigner. Aleksander was a nobleman: 'An engineer, with Paris diplomas. An officer. A veteran of the Bolshevik war. Decorated.' The peasants on the estate began to talk of confiscation, of trials and firing squads. Zoe buried her diary, and together they began to hike toward the Lithuanian border, hoping their French passports would secure them passage to England or France.

On 8 November 1939, a small notice appeared in the *Guardian*: 'News reached London yesterday that Martin Hare, the novelist, and her husband, who it was feared had lost their lives', were safe in Lithuania. Eventually, they were able to get to Sweden, where they boarded a ship destined for England. Unfortunately, soon after leaving Swedish waters, the ship was seized by a German cruiser and escorted to Lübeck, where they were thrown into a Gestapo jail. Zoe was released after a few days and allowed to travel on to Denmark, from which she gained passage to England. Aleksander disappeared.

Even when she was safe back in England, Zoe never relaxed. Whenever she went out, she wrote, 'I instinctively look for my passport and make sure it is safe. Without it I know that I am lost. Without a passport you are nothing more than a number in a concentration camp.' Knowing that her husband, if still alive, was sitting in one of those camps, she chose to publish *My Name Is Million* anonymously to protect him and their friends in Poland. In it Aleksander is referred to only as 'A'.

My Name Is Million is an account of war and flight as immediate as any news story from Ukraine, Syria or Ethiopia today. Its author did not claim to provide an objective account, only 'fragments and nightmare glimpses and words removed from almost the whole of their context and a view darkened by personal anguish'. It was, she wrote, 'A shaken kaleidoscope, true in every one of its details but not the whole picture.'

With *My Name Is Million*, Martin Hare was left behind. Zoe Zajdler, as she now preferred to be called, no longer had room for fiction in her life. She continued to hope that Poland would be liberated and that she would be reunited with Aleksander. With the help of General Władysław Sikorski and his wife, she began to collect reports of life in occupied Poland and of the exile of Poles to Siberia during the months of Soviet control of eastern Poland: 'One of the last things I heard the Polish radio say was, "Remember, all of you who are listening. Learn by heart names and places and evidence. If necessary, remember for years."'

Zoe Zajdler took on that duty of remembrance. She compiled stories of the Soviet occupation and repression and published them in *The Dark Side of the Moon* (1947), with an introduction by T. S. Eliot. This book too was published anonymously, this time to protect those mentioned from Soviet retribution. Her sole credit was a reference in the preface by General Sikorski's widow to 'a woman of scrupulous integrity and fairness'. Only when the book was reissued in 1989 was her authorship disclosed. Decades before *The Gulag Archipelago*, *The Dark Side of the Moon* revealed the horrifying details of the arrest, transport and imprisonment of those caught up in the Soviet penal system.

Zoe Zajdler's last book was a collection of Polish fairy tales published in 1959. In her introduction, she wrote that she brought to these stories 'her own memories and evocations of all these places, where their sources lie'. But she never returned to Poland and she never saw Aleksander again. He is assumed to have died in a Nazi prison or concentration camp. Zoe herself died in Kent in 1968, and so never saw the fall of the Berlin Wall and the return of an independent Poland. The Irishman I first knew as the writer of light-hearted comedies turned out, in the end, to be a woman who became a custodian of another nation's memories.

BRAD BIGELOW edits the Neglected Books website www.neglectedbooks.com and is writing a biography of the American writer and editor Virginia Faulkner.

Masefield's Magic

BRANDON ROBSHAW

I was 8 when I first read John Masefield's *The Box of Delights* – in the late 1960s, in the high-ceilinged classroom of a Victorian-built school in East London. I had not long been reading 'chapter books' as we called them, and this was the longest, most challenging and most sophisticated one I had yet encountered – and by far the most rewarding. It's not easy to convey the peculiar atmosphere of it: scary but funny; fantastical but believable; lyrical yet down-to-earth; grotesque, even nightmarish in parts, yet told in a friendly voice. Years later, when I had forgotten most of the details of the actual story and characters, the *feeling* of it remained with me, like the lingering memory of a dream.

The Box of Delights was written around the mid-point of Masefield's career, when he had been Poet Laureate for five years. It's actually a sequel to his earlier children's novel, *The Midnight Folk* (1927: see *SF* no.73), and features many of the same characters. Those who don't know these books will probably be familiar with his poems, such as the much-anthologized 'Sea Fever' ('I must go down to the seas again/ To the lonely sea and the sky . . .') and 'Cargoes' ('Quinquireme of Nineveh from distant Ophir/ Rowing home to haven in sunny Palestine . . .'). *The Box of Delights* features that same lyricism and energy. Masefield himself led an adventurous life: he ran away to sea while still a teenager and sailed all over the world; like the supertramp W. H. Davies he lived for a while as a vagrant in America,

John Masefield, *The Box of Delights* (1935)
Farshore · Pb · 400pp · £8.99 · ISBN 9781405275521

travelling and doing odd jobs; he was a medical orderly in France during the Great War; and after he had settled down with wife and children in England he led an active public life, lecturing, writing prolifically, founding the Scottish Association for the Speaking of Verse (although he was not Scottish) and taking his duties as Poet Laureate very seriously. This spirit of adventure, this restless desire to be always moving, comes through strongly in *The Box of Delights*, where the scene changes with dizzying rapidity and ranges through space and time.

The plot follows a dreamlike logic of its own. Young Kay Harker makes the acquaintance of a mysterious old Punch and Judy man, Cole Hawlings, who performs tricks of real magic and repeatedly warns Kay that 'the Wolves are Running'. To preserve his Box of Delights from falling into the hands of the Wolves, Hawlings entrusts it to Kay. The Wolves – that is to say the evil Abner Brown, his witch-wife Sylvia Pouncer and a collection of thuggish henchmen, including a disreputable Rat – spare no effort to find the box, kidnapping half of the town including all the clergymen (the Wolves want to prevent Christmas being celebrated), but they can't catch Kay, whose magic box enables him to Go Small, Go Swift and travel into the past.

But the enchanting thing about the book is not its plot but its atmosphere of magic and strangeness. It is a winter novel and most scenes are set in a snowbound landscape under a dark sky; yet because the box enables travel to other climes and times, there are frequent abrupt changes of scene, brought to life through Masefield's lyrical use of language. On page after page there are vivid images which lodge in one's mind like lines of poetry: 'a great man, antlered at the brow, dressed in deerskin and moving with the silent, slow grace of a stag'; 'The water in the bay was of the most vivid, pure green, so curiously clear that far, far below he could see shark after shark, all spotted, spangled and striped'; 'the sweet banging of a gong'; and, of course, 'the Wolves are Running'.

The gallery of characters adds to this sense of surreal strangeness. With the exception of Kay himself, who is something of a blank slate, they are all larger and weirder than life. Cole Hawlings, a bright-eyed, stooped old man with his Punch and Judy show strapped to his back, accompanied by his prancing dog Toby, is hundreds of years old and his memory stretches back a long way:

> First there were pagan times; then there were in-between times; then there were Christian times; then there was another in-between time; then there was Oliver's time; and then there was pudding-time; but there've been a lot more since then and more coming: but the time I liked best was just before the in-between time, what you might call Henry's time.

Hawlings (who is later identified as the medieval Spanish mystic, theologian and poet Ramón Lully) can conjure up a phoenix, produce forests and birds and bees and butterflies out of nowhere, and make drawings come to life.

Then there is Little Maria, Kay's cousin, a wild lawless imp of a girl in the Minnie-the-Minx mould who, before retiring, makes sure to slip some sprigs of holly into her sister's bed. When Kay hears she is coming for Christmas his reaction is: 'I do hope she has brought some pistols. She generally has one or two.' Later, Maria gets scrobbled (a lot of scrobbling goes on in the novel; it means being kidnapped, with a suggestion of comic violence). After she manages to escape, she describes her experience in these terms: 'I've been scrobbled like a greenhorn. I knew what it would be, not taking a pistol. Well, I pity them if I ever get near them again. They won't scrobble Maria Jones a second time.' Abner Brown is the mastermind behind the scrobbling; a silky voiced jewel-thief and gangster who poses as a clergyman, Dr Boddledale, and plans to double-cross all his henchpeople, including his wife (who also plans to double-cross him).

Alongside all these realist or quasi-realist figures there are mythical characters like Herne the Hunter, who takes Kay on a journey into the wild wood, where he transforms him successively into a stag, a duck and a fish.

The novel is a curious mix of the magical and the mundane. Fantasy stories are typically set in a pre-industrial world, but the world of *The Box of Delights* contains trains, telephones, telegrams and aeroplanes as well as spells and shape-shifting. Each chapter is topped and tailed by an illustration, executed in a simple cartoon style but representing surreal images, such as a rat brandishing a sword or a dancing cake-stand – as if Salvador Dalí had been commissioned to produce an issue of the *Beano*. The prose is enlivened by bursts of verse: one snatch that has stayed with me all these years is Arnold of Todi's poem about the sky, written when he was a soldier in the army of Alexander the Great: 'It arched, it arched/ We marched, we marched/ And parched and parched'. (Arnold of Todi, I should explain, is the original maker of the box, but is lost in the past; Kay visits him at the time of the Trojan War.)

It is perhaps becoming evident that this is not the sort of novel that can easily be summarized: there are too many disparate elements, too much going on. Yet it all feels as if it belongs together; everything coheres, as in a dream which makes no sense when one recounts it but makes perfect sense when one is dreaming it. The influence of *The Box of Delights* is discernible in many other classics of children's literature. The shape-shifting scenes of T. H. White's *The Sword in the Stone* are clearly inspired by Kay's transformations into stag, duck and fish. Susan Cooper's *The Dark Is Rising* features a similar sense of menace and the use of time travel, and an appearance by Herne the Hunter; and even the title feels like a nod to 'The Wolves are Running'. And I have always believed that Tove Jansson's Little My owes a good deal to Masefield's Little Maria.

Like all the best children's books, *The Box of Delights* triumphantly survives the passage into adulthood. I rediscovered it some years ago when reading it as a bedtime story to my 8-year-old daughter and was as enchanted by it as she was. And that is probably the best way to discover or rediscover it. Read it to a child. Christmastime would be best.

BRANDON ROBSHAW lectures in Children's Literature, Creative Writing and Philosophy for the Open University. He has written a Young Adult fantasy novel, *The Infinite Powers of Adam Gowers*, and a collection of children's poems, *These Are a Few of My Scariest Things*.

Unpacking My Grandparents' Books

C. J. SCHÜLER

It is one of life's ironies that when we are young, and keen to establish our own identity and place in the world, we have little interest in the experiences of older generations; by the time we come to find their stories fascinating, it is often too late. I remember my paternal grandparents as a rather severe elderly couple who, on their annual visits from Frankfurt, seemed to cast a pall of gloom over the household. After my parents' divorce we lost contact, so I had little idea of who they really were or what they had experienced in the course of their eventful lives. Then, a few years ago, I inherited a small collection of books that had belonged to them. Along with some old photo albums and other family mementos, they revealed a rich inner life.

The family were originally from Breslau (now Wrocław in Poland) but moved to Dresden in 1922. My grandfather, Alfred Schüler, was working as a lawyer for a pharmaceutical company when, in September 1935, the political situation in Germany persuaded him to take his wife Hedwig and their younger son Andreas to Barcelona. After the Spanish Civil War broke out the following year, they were forced to move once again, to Genoa, where my father joined them in 1938. After a brief return to Spain in 1939, they obtained permission to emigrate to the USA, and for eleven years Alfred worked as a night auditor at the Hotel Plymouth in New York. In 1955 he was offered a position with the United Restitution Organization, the legal aid service set up to help victims of Nazi persecution seek financial compensation from the German government. They posted him to their office in Frankfurt am Main, where – one of the few Jews to resettle in Germany after the war – he worked until his retirement in 1973.

As I unpacked the books in our London flat, blew the dust from their tops and read the inscriptions and dates on the flyleaves, I became aware that each one embodied a narrative beyond the one printed on its pages in heavy German black-letter type; that of a cosmopolitan literary and artistic culture that was obliterated in Germany by the rise of fascism but which, carried into exile, greatly enriched the wider world.

The family was not deeply observant, but here were the two volumes, bound in dark blue cloth, of my grandfather's German-language Bible, with his signature on the flyleaf over the date, '1.12.1934 (Channukah)'. It seems astonishing today that nearly two years into the Nazi regime, the Hebrew scripture could still be published in Germany (by Kauffmann Verlag), with the authority of the Jewish community of Berlin. One of its editors, Harry Torczyner, had already settled in Palestine by the time it appeared, while his colleague Georg Salzberger – a relative of my grandparents who had won the Iron Cross at Verdun – was rabbi at the liberal Westend Synagogue in Frankfurt until 1937. After a year's incarceration in Dachau, he was released and emigrated with his family to London, where he established the Belsize Square Synagogue.

The perplexities of Jewish history were represented by a three-volume set of the works of Flavius Josephus, comprising his *Antiquities of the Jews* and *History of the Jewish War*. Translated by Dr Heinrich Clementz, they were published by Benjamin Harz of Berlin and Vienna in 1923.

My grandparents were avid readers of contemporary German literature. A three-volume set of Stefan Zweig's novellas and short stories, with leather spines and marbled boards, bore my grandfather's signature on the flyleaf, along with the date 24 December 1930. By that time, the Austrian writer's books could be found on the shelves of every educated German-speaking household. In this collection, tales written over many years were retrospectively assembled into a sequence Zweig called *The Chain*, in the manner of his hero Balzac's

Comédie humaine. I had discovered Zweig's work for myself more than a decade earlier thanks to the championship of Melissa Ulfane at Pushkin Press and the superb translations of Anthea Bell (see *SF* no.6). In his haunting stories of dislocation and loss I found a world that seemed strangely familiar, like a half-remembered dream. I realize now that it was part of my cultural DNA.

Another household name at the time, though little remembered today, was Paul Heyse (1830–1914); a red clothbound three-volume set of his *Poems* (Berlin: Wilhelm Herz, 1901) had belonged to my grandmother. Heyse was an acclaimed poet, dramatist, novelist and short-story writer, whose verses were set to music by Schumann, Brahms and Hugo Wolf, and who was awarded the Nobel Prize for Literature in 1910.

Among the other major literary figures of the period, Thomas Mann was represented by his novella *Mario and the Magician*, a lovely little hardback from Fischer Verlag in a beautifully decorated slipcase. Between the pages was a bookmark from the Dresden bookseller G. A. Kaufmann, and on the flyleaf was pencilled the date 7.6.1930.

Soft maroon leather blocked with rich gold lettering encased a German translation (by H. Bock-Neumann) of Jens Peter Jacobsen's *Niels Lyhne.* One of the most celebrated works of Danish fiction, and much admired by Thomas Mann, this 1880 novel tells of a young poet's struggle to make sense of his existence. On the flyleaf, over the date 'Am 26 Mai 1911', was written a quotation from Nietzsche's *Thus Spoke Zarathustra*:

O my soul, I have given thee everything, and all my hands have become empty by thee – and now! Now sayest thou to me, smiling and full of melancholy: 'Which of us oweth thanks? – Doth the giver not owe thanks because the receiver received? Is bestowing not a necessity? Is receiving not – pitying?'

Then there was an antiquarian curio, *A Description and History of the Bastille during the Reigns of Louis XIV, XV and XVI*, translated from the French and published by Herold Bros of Hamburg in 1790. The book was a gift to my grandfather from a friend: on the flyleaf was inscribed, 'To my dear Dr Schüler, as a lasting memento of E. M. Simon, July 1933'.

There were also many of the slim hardbacks produced by the Leipzig publisher Insel-Verlag which, according to Allen Lane, provided the inspiration for the King Penguin format. Launched in 1912, the series was instantly recognizable by its stiff cardboard bindings covered with bold patterned paper, on to which a label was pasted bearing the author's name and the title. Among my grandparents' collection were the very first of the series, Rilke's prose poem *The Love and Death of Cornet Christoph Rilke*, Hugo von Hofmannsthal's verse drama *The Fool and Death* and Zweig's *Decisive Moments of Mankind*, a collection of five 'historical miniatures' ranging from the Battle of Waterloo to the California Gold Rush.

I was surprised by the number of miniature volumes my grandparents possessed, until it occurred to me that their portability enabled them to survive the frequent jettisoning of personal effects that must accompany a life in exile. They included a handful of tiny books from the Zwickau publisher Schumann Brothers' 'Portable Library of Italian Classics': two marble-bound volumes containing Giovanni Battista Guarini's *The Faithful Shepherd* (1819), along with one-volume editions of Giuseppe Parini's satirical poem 'The Day' and Tasso's *Selected Poems* (both printed in 1821). The Berlin publisher Friedberg & Mode's 'Théâtre Français' collection contributed a miniature edition of Molière's *Le Malade imaginaire*, while the English-language titles included a tiny *Merry Wives of Windsor* bound in orange leather and – between tartan boards – Sir Walter Scott's *The Lady of the Lake*, both published by David Bryce & Sons of Glasgow.

It didn't seem right to keep all these books myself – though I would hang on to the Zweig and a few others – so I posted some to my cousin in Hawaii, a painstaking and indefatigable researcher to whom I owe much of my knowledge of family history. Others, along with a couple of the photo albums, I decided to deliver in person when I next visited another cousin in Dresden. I took the Eurostar to Brussels, and then the Thalys train to Cologne, where I spent the night in an old-fashioned hotel overlooking the Rhine. Carnival was in full swing.

From Cologne, I travelled via Frankfurt, Fulda and Leipzig to Dresden; nearly thirty years after reunification, west–east train journeys in Germany can still be circuitous. As the train crossed the bridge over the Elbe, a Baroque symphony of cupolas and pinnacles unfolded. When I first visited, only a few stumpy towers arose from the blackened ruins; now, virtually the entire historic skyline has been recreated. My cousin met me at the Hauptbahnhof and drove me the short distance to her flat. After supper, I brought out the books, including several of the colourful Insel titles, and photo albums. My cousin and her husband were particularly captivated by the photos taken by my father on visits to them, which conjured back into being the lost world of the GDR: the street signs, the lamp-posts, the Trabants.

The next morning, we took the tram to the Altstadt. In front of the Frauenkirche, the great domed church destroyed in the Allied bombing raid of February 1945 and painstakingly reconstructed between 1994 and 2005, three red buses had been set on end. Used to ferry Syrian civilians from Aleppo before it fell to Assad's forces the previous autumn, they now formed an installation by the artist Manaf Halbouni. Entitled *Monument*, it was a message from one war-ravaged city to another, and a stark reminder that the saga of exile and loss is far from over.

C. J. SCHÜLER explores more of his family history in his book *Along the Amber Route: From St Petersburg to Venice*, which was shortlisted for the Stanford-Dolman Travel Book of the Year and is available from Sandstone Press.

Bibliography

Anon. [Lucy Zoe Girling Zajdler], *My Name Is Million* — 80

Robert Bringhurst, *The Elements of Typographic Style* — 59

Michael Cox, *The Meaning of Night*; *The Glass of Time* — 18

Martin Crawford, *Creating a Forest Garden* — 24

Alastair Fitter & David More, *Trees* — 24

F. W. Holiday, *The Great Orm of Loch Ness* — 37

Nella Last's War: The Second World War Diaries of Housewife, 49 — 12

Rose Macaulay, *The World My Wilderness* — 41

Nadezhda Mandelstam, *Hope against Hope*; *Hope Abandoned* — 31

John Masefield, *The Box of Delights* — 85

Thomas Pakenham, *Meetings with Remarkable Trees* — 24

C. J. Schüler: on inheriting his grandparents' books — 90

R. C. Sherriff, *The Fortnight in September* — 7

Muriel Spark, *The Prime of Miss Jean Brodie* — 63

The Stanley Letters — 53

Chris Starr, *Woodland Management* — 24

Henri Troyat, *Tolstoy* — 47

H. G. Wells, *The War of the Worlds* — 67

Florence White, *Good Things in England* — 73

Peter Wohlleben, *The Hidden Life of Trees* — 24

Coming attractions

FELICITY JAMES takes tea in Cranford · TOM HODGKINSON
escapes to Kirrin Island · DEREK PARKER meets a prince and a showgirl ·
FLORA WATKINS acts as a go-between · ADAM FOULDS reads *The Book of
Disquiet* · PAMELA BEASANT visits a bookshop in Stromness · ANDREW
JOYNES follows a snow goose